PRAISE FOR *Before y*

D0005588

"Are you desperately, passionately in love? Are you convinced that you've met your 'knight in shining armor' or your beautiful 'princess bride?' Before you take the next step, you *must* read this book. Why? Because far too many love-struck couples get engaged without taking the time to seriously consider if: 1) they are truly ready for marriage; and 2) the person they are dating will make a good marriage partner.

Dave Gudgel is committed to helping you enter into engagement with your eyes wide open. He wants you to have the vital, life-long marriage that God intends for you to have. So, before you get engaged —get this book!"

Dr. Bill Maier, Vice President and
Psychologist in Residence, Focus on the Family

"Wow, this book is the total package! Not only is it a primer for what a healthy marriage should look like, it offers insight from a wise counselor and the almost engaged. Anyone considering marriage would benefit from this book. Thanks Gudgels!"

Bill Butterworth, Popular Author & Speaker

"*Before You Get Engaged* addresses life priorities that can sometimes get a little out of whack in what my best friend calls the 'initial love fog.' It asks valid questions, questions that come from others that have already been married and divorced. How is my relationship better or more solid than theirs? It made me feel okay for having the same questions. It's a very exciting and somewhat scary time, not in a bad way, but in a way that you just want the very best for you and this person that you love. Enticing, encouraging, and an easy read, it was engagement from a different, very positive perspective. I can't wait for my guy to read it!"

Jorden, Age 26, Dallas, TX

"We would recommend this book to anyone who is thinking about getting engaged. This book serves as a great catalyst for conversation about the complex feelings and concerns surrounding engagement and marriage. After reading this book we both feel confident about our getting engaged and are more than excited about our future together."

Elizabeth & Adam, Age 25, Phoenix, AZ

"This book really helped me as I'm currently going through a difficult transition out of a three year relationship. Brent and Danielle's story gave me the hope and encouragement to move forward and put God back at the center of my life."

Corey, Age 28, Los Angeles, CA

"As a graduate student in a serious relationship, this book was a blessing from God. For the past two years I have been seeking God's direction concerning potential marriage possibilities with my girlfriend. This book has been the answer to my prayers. It is fascinating, easy to read, and incredibly entertaining. Mixing biblical truth with personal stories spoke volumes into my life and was extremely helpful as I was able to relate to many of the thoughts, feelings, and situations presented. I truly believe I am better prepared to move forward in my relationship as a result of reading this book. Seeking God's guidance and remaining faithful to Him, I look forward to great things to come."

Peter, Age 25, Lynchburg, VA

"Neither of us knew the questions that needed to be asked and answered before getting engaged, however, we knew that marriage was our ultimate goal. *Before You Get Engaged* helped us individually—and together as a couple—look inward to realize what we need to do and be prior to becoming engaged, outward at the experience of others who openly share their stories, and most importantly upward at God's biblical counsel to His children. Pastor Dave and Brent Gudgel, your book could not have come at a better time for us."

Brian & Michelle, Age 39 & 29, Phoenix, AZ

"*Before You Get Engaged* is an insightful book that emphasizes the emotional, physical, and spiritual completion one must have before considering engagement. In every chapter Gudgel intertwines personal stories along with a side commentary from his son Brent and girlfriend Danielle who are considering engagement. Through these stories the reader can easily relate to the complications that emerge in serious relationships. Not only does Gudgel include important questions, he provides a series of answers in order for all couples to discover their own unique response. Although I am not personally in a relationship, after reading this book I now know what to look for, question, and confirm in the future when I do find that special someone."

May, Age 18, Phoenix, AZ

"This book is a must read for anyone in a serious dating relationship! (Another possible title could be *While You Are Dating*.) The insight of Brent and Danielle—and their willingness to share their experiences as a couple, along with their interaction with each chapter—was especially helpful and relevant to my own dating relationship. Dave's writing is not only fun to read, he gets to the heart of each topic addressed."

Becca, Age 26, La Mirada, CA

"My boyfriend and I have searched for the right book to prepare us for engagement with no success. I am so glad that we discovered this one! It is a must read for a couple that is dating and thinking about engagement. It was extremely beneficial. It not only reinforced the importance of God being the center of the relationship—before taking that next step to engagement—but offered advice and insight that every couple should consider."

Sally, Age 25, Memphis, TN

BEFORE YOU GET
Engaged

David R. Gudgel
Brent Gudgel

with Danielle Fitch

THOMAS NELSON
Since 1798

NASHVILLE   DALLAS   MEXICO CITY   RIO DE JANEIRO

© 2007 David R. Gudgel

All rights reserved. No portion of this book may be reproduced, stored in a retrieval system, or transmitted in any form or by any means—electronic, mechanical, photocopy, recording, scanning, or other—except for brief quotations in critical reviews or articles, without the prior written permission of the publisher.

Published in Nashville, Tennessee, by Thomas Nelson. Thomas Nelson is a registered trademark of Thomas Nelson, Inc.

Thomas Nelson, Inc. titles may be purchased in bulk for educational, business, fund-raising, or sales promotional use. For information, please e-mail SpecialMarkets@ThomasNelson.com.

All Scripture quotations, unless otherwise indicated, are taken from The Holy Bible, New International Version (NIV). ©1973, 1978, 1984, International Bible Society. Used by permission of Zondervan Bible Publishers.

Page Design by Casey Hooper

Library of Congress Cataloging-in-Publication Data
Gudgel, David R.
    Before you get engaged / David R. Gudgel, Brent Gudgel, with Danielle Fitch.
        p. cm.
    Includes bibliographical references.
    ISBN 978-0-8499-1918-3 (pbk.)
    1. Mate selection. 2. Mate selection—Religious aspects—Christianity. 3. Betrothal—Decision making. 4. Betrothal—Religious aspects—Christianity. 5. Man-woman relationships. 6. Man-woman relationships—Religious aspects—Christianity. 1. Gudgel, Brent. 11. Fitch, Danielle. 111. Title.
HQ801.G783 2007
241'.6765—dc22

                                                                                    2007025658

Printed in the United States of America
09 10 11 12 WC 11 10 9

Contents

Acknowledgments

Thanks a lot!

Bill, thanks for asking the question that got this whole project going.

John, thanks for your encouragement and help in getting this book published.

Steve, thanks for being the best and only agent I have ever had.

Bernice, thanks for all you did to make the book better than it would have been.

Brian and Mary, thanks for helping me see the need for writing the book.

Brent, thanks for making this book a ten.

Katie, thanks in advance for using this book before you get engaged.

Danielle, thanks for your willingness to share your story. It would be great to have you become a Gudgel, but however this journey ends, you're an incredible girl, and we love you!

The one hundred-plus couples who took the survey, thanks for taking the time to share your engagement stories.

Introduction
THINKING ABOUT ENGAGEMENT?

*H*ad I not been put on the spot, this book may have never been written. The idea for *Before You Get Engaged* started during a radio interview I did with *Focus on the Family*. For the most part, my interview with Focus vice president and psychologist Bill Maier and radio host John Fuller went pretty well. We were talking about my book *Before You Live Together,* which shows why a couple is better off waiting until after marriage to live together.

In the middle of the broadcast, Bill asked me to talk about the importance of premarital counseling. For twenty-five years I had seen firsthand the value of a premarital ministry for couples who are engaged to be married, so I had a lot to say about its importance. I did my best to stress the need for every church to have a ministry to help engaged couples prepare for marriage.

But then Dr. Maier insightfully said, "I almost think that it's counterproductive to do the premarital counseling when the wedding is two months out . . . I personally believe it needs to occur perhaps just before the engagement . . . that's the time to really look at these issues. Before you've reserved the church, you've got the photographer, you've ordered the invitations, and spent a lot of money on rings. At that point you have such a commitment, it's a lot harder to say, 'You know what? This isn't right.' I'm thinking that preengagement counseling rather than premarital counseling in many cases could actually be more effective. Dave, what do you think?"[1]

That's when I felt on the spot. The first thing that came to my mind was, "Huh?" I had never even heard of such a thing. I had the feeling that "Huh?" was not the right response, so I kind of stumbled through an attempt at an answer. I said, "Well, Bill, I think that would be great, but that's going to start a new trend, because we as pastors don't do that. We don't have this kind of ministry in our church. I think what you're saying is really important and maybe it is something that I personally should be considering in terms of our ministry. But across the nation, I think what you're suggesting is something that is absent in ministry."

Since that interview, the more I've thought about Bill's words, the more I agree. While helping a couple after engagement is important, helping them before engagement can be even better.

Dr. Maier was a gracious host. After my rambling reply, he let me off the hook and moved on to a new subject. But God didn't. In the days, weeks, and months that followed our interview, I couldn't get Bill's words off my mind. Those thoughts all crystallized when one of my sons began getting very serious with his girlfriend.

Mary and Brian met while attending Azusa Pacific University in Southern California. What began as a friendship ultimately grew into a dating relationship. After dating for a couple of months, the time came for Brian to "meet the parents." If the tension of driving *forever* through L.A.'s rush-hour traffic to get to the Macaroni Grill where her parents would meet them wasn't enough, the tension of hoping to make a good first impression made this a scary occasion for Brian. The pressure multiplied when the waiter asked him, "the new boyfriend," to write a poem on the paper tablecloth (which is typical décor, along with crayons, in a Macaroni Grill) about Mary. Brian later told me, "Talk about pressure. It was the first time the word *boyfriend* was used in our relationship and my first time with Mary's parents. I felt like I was about to make it or break it right there."

Call it divine inspiration or desperation, Brian quickly jotted down these words:

To the most amazing girl in the world.
You're worth all the traffic it took to get here
and there's nobody else I'd rather sit in it with.

Ka-ching! Brian's first-impression credits jumped up. Almost a zero—now a hero. His spur-of-the-moment poem went over really well. Even the waiter gave him a high five. With the blessing of Mary's parents, Brian and Mary left that dinner excited about what the future might hold for them as a couple.

After several more months of dating, Brian and Mary reached the point many couples do. They started talking about the possibility of marriage. When I got word of that, Bill's comment about the importance of churches having a preengagement ministry hit me like a ton of bricks. I wanted to do whatever I could to help Brian and Mary ask and answer some very important questions before they got engaged. I remember wishing I had a book like this one that could help them figure out if they should move ahead with their relationship.

Ultimately they came to the point where they felt sure that marriage was the right thing for them to do, although they will tell you that they would have loved to have a book like this to help them make that important decision. Fortunately they are now happily married and doing well, with those engagement and marriage decisions behind them.

Around the time of Brian and Mary's wedding, I learned that my other son, Brent, was in a relationship where he was faced with his own preengagement decision. He was trying to decide if he and his girlfriend, Danielle, should get engaged. As I realized their relationship had gotten to this point, I once again wished I had a book like this one to help them process the direction their relationship was taking. So I decided it was time to write that book.

I also asked Brent and Danielle if they would be willing to help me by:

- reading the chapters as I wrote them,
- processing the principles in their own lives and relationship, and
- making comments that could be included in the book.

They agreed. And as you will see in the pages that follow, they truly are trying to sort out if engagement and marriage is right for them as a couple.

In the first three parts of this book, I give couples like Brent and Danielle twelve things to consider before they get engaged. The first part focuses on whether each of you *personally* is ready to be married. The second part will help you decide if you *as a couple* are ready to get engaged and ultimately married. In the third part I ask you to consider the input of three significant others before you make your engagement decision.

Hopefully, if you process through the principles in the first three parts of this book, you will come to one of three decisions regarding your relationship. The fourth part of this book will then help you act on the decision you make.

Along the way, you will be reading Brent's firsthand pre-engagement thoughts and comments. I think you will find his input extremely practical and valuable. Danielle has also made some contributions that you will find honest and helpful. I am really excited for both of them and grateful for their willingness to share their journey with us.

◉ BRENT

In my twenty-something years on this planet, I've learned the following about commitment:

- Making the right commitment is preferable to the wrong commitment.
- Always consult God if you want to make the right commitment.

Sure, these both might be obvious, but for some reason I often find them being easier said than done. In this book I'll try to do my best at being honest. I'll be adding "color commentary" by making statements like the ones above. I'll share observations. I'll share stories (all of which will most likely be genius in nature). I'll do my best to keep my comments simple and practical. But please don't expect anything more. If you want more, read the bulk of this book or a Bible dictionary.

I'm a young filmmaker and writer who happened to be considering engagement while his father was writing a book about engagement. I'm going into this book thinking I probably want to get engaged in the coming months, but I'm realizing it is important to take a step back and really think it through. I don't want to make the wrong commitment (even if I already think engagement is the right choice).

When one makes a wrong choice about engagement, it's hard to stop the impending wedding. And if one makes a wrong choice about marriage, it just messes everything up. Often when things in a marriage are messed up, people get divorced. For me, divorce is not an option. Divorce is bad.

For the sake of discussion, I did some research on divorce (and by *research* I mean Wikipedia) and came up with the following conclusion: *Maybe people who get divorced shouldn't have gotten married.* Sure, this is simplifying way too much, but in every circumstance, I believe this "advice" probably would have solved the problem.

I love Danielle. It makes me smile to think of marrying her. But I don't want to make a wrong decision. So since I know it doesn't hurt to ask, I'm going into this book asking the question, "Should Danielle and I get engaged to be married?"

Ultimately my hope is that I will help you connect with God and His Word. Each principle in the pages that follow is based upon the Bible, which I consider essential for a solid relationship now and after marriage. Along with the Scriptures, I have also surveyed the preengagement experiences of more than one hundred couples. Their practical experiences illustrate why the principles in this book are absolutely essential to consider before you get engaged.

Years ago Ann Landers reported the results of an informal

poll she took among her readers. Her question "If you had to do it all over again, would you marry the same person?" drew an avalanche of replies. Shockingly, 70 percent said no, they would not marry the person they had married.[2] Recently AOL, in conjunction with *Woman's Day* magazine, asked a similar question of women: "If you had to do it all over again, would you marry the same husband?" Thirty-six percent said no, 20 percent said they weren't sure, and 44 percent said yes.[3]

As a pastor who has done a lot of counseling, I've heard a husband or wife say the same thing on more than one occasion. They regret having married the person they did. I think that feeling is preventable, and I believe the best time to prevent that from ever being said is before marriage. Even before engagement. My prayer is that whatever the future holds for you, this book will help you be sure that you are getting engaged, and ultimately married, to the right person.

Part 1

ARE YOU SURE YOU'RE READY?

One

● WOULD YOU MARRY YOU?

*I*f you ever want to confront someone, I would advise having him sit on the end of a diving board fully clothed, with his legs dangling over the water. Then all you have to do is sit next to him so that you're blocking his access to land. This way he has no escape unless he wants to get wet and look stupid. My mom taught me this. She revealed this clever trick as she coerced me onto the end of a diving board, blocking my escape, and exclaimed, "David, you know I love you, right?"

This is one of the worst phrases you can hear at the beginning of a conversation. I wanted to leave. Little did I know that this conversation on the diving board would change the rest of my life.

I had just begun my freshman year at Fresno City College in the same way I had finished my three years at Hoover High School: I was right back on the road to academic mediocrity. A few months earlier, I had graduated from high school with a 1.99 GPA. I was an underachiever. God had given me a good mind; I just wasn't using it.

My mom knew my potential. That's why she met me late one afternoon at the front door.

"David Ray," she said, "you and I need to go out into the backyard and talk. Right now!"

I preferred my mom calling me Dave rather than David or David Ray. When she called me Dave, I knew whatever she was going to say was no big deal. David could go either way on the good or bad scale. But David Ray always meant the same thing: trouble was coming my way. A David Ray moment was never good.

Mom led me out into the backyard.

"David," she said, "I want you to go over there and sit down on our diving board."

"OK," I said, "but can we make this fast? I have things to do."

"Just be quiet and go over there and sit down."

I went and sat on the diving board. She came and sat down next to me, which forced me farther out over the water.

So there I was, stuck on the diving board with no chance of escape. My mom was quite smart and she knew it as she looked me right in the eyes and uttered that dreaded line, "David, you know I love you, right?"

"Yes, Mom."

"Well I can see you've begun your college education the same way you finished high school. I care too much about you to let you do *this* all over again."

Mom didn't have to clarify the *this*. I knew what she was

talking about. Call *this* what you want—going through the motions, just getting by, slacking, lack of effort—anyway you look at it, she knew I was still sloughing off at school.

"Yes, Mom."

"David, if you don't buckle down and change, you're going to waste your life. Is that what you want to do?"

"No, Mom."

"Well then, you better do something about it."

I have no idea how many Mom-to-David-Ray conversations I've had over the years, but I do know this: the diving board discussion stuck. It changed me. I look back on it as a defining moment in my life. It was the kick in the posterior I needed to get on track toward realizing my full potential. After that discussion, not only did my attitude toward academics change, but so did other areas of my life.

Shortly after Mom and I talked, I had a long conversation with God about where my life was headed. A year prior, I had made a spiritual commitment to do better with my life in the future than I had in the past. God used Mom on that diving board to put more *academic action* into that decision. But I was also feeling God leading me to do something about the other areas of my life that also needed a makeover.

Academically, I buckled down and started to get better grades. I actually began to enjoy going to school and trying to do my best. Socially, I made an intentional decision to stop dating girls. Up to that point, I had been on a four-year dating run.

◉ BRENT

BRENT: Ha-ha. I didn't know this. Did you say you were dating God?

DAD: No, that's ridiculous. You can't date God.

BRENT: That's true, but when I was in college, I went for a time (length to remain undisclosed) without a date and started telling people it was because I was dating God. The funny thing is, as soon as I told people I was "dating my Lord and Savior," I started having all these girls wanting to hang out with me. They said they were also dating God!

Actually, I'm totally kidding. I've never told anyone I was dating God, though I really did take some time off.

DAD: You're so cynical. Where did I go wrong?

BRENT: Sorry. Actually, I know this "time off" can be a good idea. Sorry for joking. It's a serious book and a serious chapter.

For me, if I was going to get my act together, I needed to stop dating for a time and figure out what I wanted out of this area of my life. I also took a close look at my career path. My personal life also had several rough edges in it. I had some unresolved issues that needed to be addressed and made right.

Looking back, my diving-board discussion with Mom and the decisions and changes I made over the next year ultimately made me a better person. I became someone who I not only could like, but others could like too. In fact, after I got on the road to becoming the right person myself, I found Bernice. My relationship with her would probably never have happened had I not gotten my life together the previous year.

❍ BRENT

As Danielle and I try to figure out this whole engagement and marriage thing, there are hard questions I need to ask about my relationship with Danielle. I need to know if she's ready, but first I guess it makes sense that I should look at myself and ask, "Am *I* ready to get married?"

It's a huge question. Would I marry myself or want someone to marry me? Am I ready to get married? 'Cause if not, I need to know

now and I need to figure out how to get ready. So I'll start by first asking the question, as my dad put it, "Would I marry myself?"

SOMETHING'S MISSING

For several years now, Drs. Les and Leslie Parrott have taught a course on relationships at Seattle Pacific University. Every time they teach this popular course, they begin the first class with this sentence: "If you try to find intimacy with another person before achieving a sense of identity on your own, all your relationships become an attempt to complete yourself."[1] In their book *Relationships,* they go on to say, "Most of us tell ourselves, 'If I find the right person, my life will be complete'. . . . The truth is, the cause of our emptiness is not a case of missing persons in our lives, but a case of incompletion in our soul. In order to build healthy relationships, you must be well on your way to becoming whole or complete."[2]

A dating or engagement relationship, or ultimately a marriage, is only as healthy as the health of the individuals in it. Relational health is vitally connected to individual health. Abigail found that out the hard way.

MARRIED TO A FOOL

The Bible tells us about a woman named Abigail who married Nabal, who was a fool. You have to wonder if she knew *fool* was what his name meant literally when she married him, or if she found out about his foolishness the hard way. One thing is for sure, Nabal proved just how *full of foolishness* he was when he told ten of King David's men to take a hike after they had asked him for some food. His insulting response pretty much typified how the Bible describes him. On the one hand, he was incredibly rich, but on the other hand, he was harsh, evil, and worthless. Was he teachable? Hardly. Those who knew him said, "No one can talk to him."[3]

Abigail stood out in vivid contrast. She was intelligent, beautiful, and discerning.[4] On one occasion, after her husband had scorned David and his family, she single-handedly was able to prevent David and his army from an avenging slaughter of Nabal and everybody else connected to him.[5] But that couldn't undo Nabal's personhood. Even Abigail said he was worthless.[6] Tragically, Nabal never got it together, relationally or otherwise, before his life was abruptly ended by a heart attack.[7]

Abigail was relationally strong and healthy. Nabal epitomized a lack of health, which inflicted damage on all of his relationships. I'd like to think that each one of us can steer clear of that kind of relational damage if we are willing to pay attention to the personal issues that are keeping us from living in health.

THE PATHWAY TO PERSONAL HEALTH

Neil Clark Warren and Les Parrott have said in their excellent book *Love the Life You Live,* that personal health and wholeness have three hallmarks:[8]

1. A right relationship with God—your purpose for living and the power to change is grounded in God's unconditional love.
2. A right relationship with others—you sacrificially love others by willingly meeting their needs.
3. A right relationship with yourself—you know who you are and live in congruence with your personality and God-given talents.

Warren and Parrott, along with others who have studied human behavior, weren't the first to suggest that these three relationships are essential signs of health. Years ago, Jesus Himself boiled the essence of personal health down to these same three relationships when he summarized God's relational design this way: "'Love the Lord your God with all your heart and with all your soul and with all your mind and with all your strength'. The second is this: 'Love your neighbor as yourself.' There is no commandment greater than these."[9] Personal health is vitally connected to our relationships with God, others, and ourselves.

I like to think of my life as having gauges. My first car lacked *intelligent* gauges. Instead my dashboard had what has been fondly, or not so fondly, called *idiot lights*. Evidently, car makers had decided that most drivers were too stupid to be able to read oil and coolant gauges, so they installed a light to come on *after* a problem had already occurred. From my perspective, that's idiocy, because it keeps you from monitoring the gauges and doing something about a possible problem before it becomes critical.[10] For three years I put up with idiot lights in my first car, but when I purchased my second car, I made sure it had at least three critical dashboard gauges—an oil pressure gauge, an engine coolant gauge, and a charging system gauge. After I learned how to read those gauges, I was able to steer clear of what could have been big car problems in the five years I owned that car.

CHECK YOUR GAUGES

When Socrates said, "Know thyself," he was not only quoting one of the "seven sages" of ancient Greece, he was declaring that an unexamined life is not worth living.[11] Several years later, the apostle Paul wrote, "Pay close attention to yourself."[12]

One of the ways you can do that is by paying close attention to the three most important gauges in your life. Are they indicating an empty or full tank? Do you need to do something about any or all of these areas of your life? Here are a few things to look for as you consider how full these gauges are in your life.

The Spiritual Gauge

When I meet someone new to me, besides asking them the usual questions like, where do you work? are you in school? where do you live? do you have a family? I like to ask people, do you have any spiritual beliefs? That simple question has opened the door to many significant spiritual conversations. You know what I've found? Most people's spiritual tanks aren't even close to being full. Their spiritual gauges would register just above empty.

I agree with St. Augustine, who prayed, "Everlasting God, in whom we live and move and have our being: You have made us for Yourself, and our hearts are restless until they rest in You."[13] I believe this life is ultimately not going to make sense until we get connected to God in a personal way. I like the image Paul uses when he prays that his readers would be filled up with "the *fullness* of God."[14] Jesus had the same thing in mind when He said, "I have come that they may have life, and have it to the *full*."[15]

If your spiritual gauge is registering anything less than full in your relationship with God, I'd strongly suggest you talk to a pastor, a friend, or someone who can help you get this part of your life sorted out. It's way too important to ignore. Personally I believe anyone who makes a God connection through Jesus Christ will never be the same. And that's good. God's power released in you will begin to produce qualities like love, joy, peace, patience, kindness, goodness, faithfulness, gentleness, and self-control.[16] Those are the qualities of which a great personal life and strong relationships are made.

● BRENT

In the last six months, two of my guy friends have gotten divorced. They are in their early to midtwenties. Already my friends are getting divorced? I couldn't believe it when I first heard. How could this happen?

When I found out about their divorces, fear quickly crept into my mind. I worried, *If they got divorced, does that mean I could? 'Cause they both thought their marriages would last.*

But then I started finding out more details, and it became apparent why the divorce happened in both cases. At least, it was apparent to me. I'm not talking about why they ultimately said they were getting divorced, but what I think was at the core of both situations: they were trying to find fulfillment in their relationships. In both cases—whether they were unhappy or a spouse left for someone else—the problem started when someone was looking for fulfillment apart from God.

When a relationship is great and you're in love, of course you find happiness in being with the other person. I've found that with Danielle, and it's wonderful. The problem, though, is when this happiness becomes the driving force of our relationship.

So I ask myself, "Am I with Danielle because I want her to fulfill me?" No. Danielle and I have actually talked about this and we both acknowledge that we can't ultimately fulfill the other, even though we do want to make each other happy. But we know if we're not happy or fulfilled apart, on our own, we won't ultimately be happy together. Maybe for a time, but not a long time (i.e., the rest of our lives).

I think the pursuit of God, individually first and then together as a couple, is the healthy way. So now I have to figure out how to do that.

The Relational Gauge

The relational gauge, maybe more than any other gauge, will reveal how healthy you are. In fact, the Bible goes so far as to say, "The entire law is summed up in a single command: 'Love your neighbor as yourself.'"[17] Everything boils down to the love you have for others. The love referred to here, which is *agape* love in Greek, goes way beyond sexual love or the love of friendship. This is the love of sacrifice. It shows up in relationships when people don't deserve it.

Once again the goal is to be *full* of love, but this time toward others. Paul realized how important this love is when he said to his friends at Thessalonica: "May the Lord make your love increase and *overflow* for each other and for everyone else, just as ours does for you."[18] When this love is full in a person's life, patience and kindness will prevail. Feelings of jealousy will be done away with. Arrogance and rudeness will be absent. Unselfishness will be prominent. Unrighteous anger won't rear its ugly head. Unmerited forgiveness will be extended. This kind of love won't give in, or give up, or quit giving out.[19]

Sounds too good to be true, doesn't it? Actually, if this love was dependent on you or me, its fullness would never be realized in our lives. But as Paul said, you can increase in the fullness of love through God's work in you.

Here's what you want to look for on your relational gauge:

1. *Are you a person who loves others more than, or at least as much as, yourself?* If not, you have some growing to do before you're ready to be in a serious relationship.
2. *Is the direction of your life moving toward the qualities of*

love described above? Don't get hung up on perfection, but do look for direction. Are you becoming a more loving person?

3. *Have you forgiven those who've hurt you in the past?* If you haven't, they are continuing to hurt you even now and will affect your present relationships.

Look at your spiritual gauge again. It's been said, "We cannot love until we first experience love."[20] The relational gauge with God and the relational love gauge with others are vitally connected. You can't have one without the other. But when both are increasing, you are going to be well on your way to being a healthy person.

The Identity Gauge

There's a big difference between "being full of yourself" and "realizing your full potential." The first comes out of an unhealthy heart that's full of pride and arrogance. The second rises out of a grateful and accepting heart. You need to be full of the latter or you will fall into a "compulsion for completion" trap.[21]

Authors Les and Leslie Parrott are right on track when they say, "If we have not achieved a solid sense of who we are . . . we are destined to believe one of two subtle lies guaranteed to sabotage our relationships: (1) I need this person to be complete, and (2) if this person needs me, I'll be complete."[22] These feelings in turn can compel a woman to ask, "Am I desirable?" and a man to ask, "Am I capable?"[23] This unhealthy focus will eventually hurt you, because your identity is grounded in others' approval, acceptance, and recognition. But you won't consistently receive that approval, especially when you blow it and let others down.

Your identity, instead, needs to be solely attached to your identity in Christ, which is not based on *what* you do but on *who* you are. It's not based on others' acceptance of you; it's based on God's acceptance of you. If you have a personal relationship with God through Christ, you are, and always will be, accepted. You have potential and purpose. You begin to see yourself as God sees you: a person with intrinsic value, placed on planet Earth at this time in history to make a significant difference. To bring honor to God through your life and lips. Do you believe that?

The fullness of your identity tank is not found in thinking "of yourself more highly than you ought, but rather think[ing] of yourself with sober judgment, in accordance with the measure of faith God has given you."[24] Chances are, if you are looking to your accomplishments or others for approval, your identity gauge is constantly bouncing all over the place. You may be an emotional basket case. You'll be better off when you calm your identity gauge by stabilizing yourself in who God has made you to be. He alone, as the God of hope, can *"fill you with all joy and peace as you trust in him, so that you may overflow with hope by the power of the Holy Spirit."*[25] Simply stated, the fullness of hope, joy, peace, and power in this life are not found in playing to the crowd but in accepting who God made you to be and living to please Him.

◉ BRENT

A few months ago, after reading Dad's first draft of this chapter, I went on a quest to find an answer to the big question, "Would I marry myself?" I started processing this through intangible things like prayer and just thinking about it. From that experience, here's what I recommend:

Pursue God. I started out by making sure I was pursuing God. This you can't measure, though. I just had to pursue Him and ask if I was finding my pleasure and fulfillment in Him. I've realized it doesn't end when I ask the question, because it's a continual process. I have to be daily asking this and daily seeking to follow God.

But that's not new. Those of us who grew up in the church know this; we just don't necessarily take it to heart. So I will also recommend a few other things I did that helped me figure stuff out:

Get a mentor. This is a big deal for me. I didn't have one before and always knew I probably should have someone older and wiser speaking into my life. I used to pray for this. I would ask God for a mentor and then sit and wait and wonder why He never provided one. Then one day I realized maybe God wanted me to do something about it. I asked an older and wiser man I respected if he'd be interested in mentoring me—and he said yes. It was that easy. All I had to do was be proactive, and now I have someone who prods me in the areas I need to improve. I tell him about my goals and the issues in my life, and he asks the hard questions to guide me along the way.

Go to counseling. I don't particularly like to divulge my baggage to the world, but I'll admit it: I went to counseling. There were a few things in my life I wanted to make sure weren't issues and, if they were, that I wasn't going to bring them into a marriage. I kind of just wanted a shrink to tell me I was OK and good to get engaged. It was a very revealing process, where I talked through fears and struggles, hopes and dreams with a professional. I can't believe I just wrote that, but it's true. I went to counseling, and I would recommend it to everyone before making this kind of decision.

Spend time apart. A significant amount of time. Danielle went to Ethiopia for a month and I went to Rwanda. Both of us were taking trips for work reasons (missions-related) and, incredibly, it worked out so we were gone at exactly the same time. I know the Lord worked this timing out, because it was too perfect. Being apart from each other allowed us to think through things: I could ask questions like, *Am I happy apart from Danielle?* and, *Am I looking for my fulfillment in her?* and even, *Do I really miss her and really love her?* It was an unbelievable month for both of us. We grew a ton while apart, and learned so much about our relationship. And yes, we figured out we were happy when apart, and the joy from our relationship together was a gift.

Plus, our time apart really told me something when I picked her up at the airport. I had knots in my stomach and sweaty palms from being so nervous. Then when she walked around the corner at customs, my smile was as big as the day I first fell in love with her. I learned I wasn't looking for my fulfillment in her, but I realized how much I cared for and was committed to her. It was all incredibly revealing.

I realize that just because that's how I did it doesn't mean that's how everyone should. Not everyone can go off to a foreign country. But however you figure it out, it has to start with the pursuit of God. Pray lots. Then be proactive and do something. Don't just wait around. Do whatever you need to do to answer the question, *Am I ready to get married?*

And by the way, if you're scared to ask that question or afraid of what the answer might be, then you definitely need to ask the question.

◉ DANIELLE

" . . . the cheerful sound of birds singing and wedding bells ringing could be heard throughout the land as Prince Charming took the beautiful princess into his arms and kissed her. As the sun set over their happy kingdom, their hearts were filled with joy. And they lived happily ever after." The End

Over the time I've been with Brent, I've gotten to know and

love him deeply. It's exciting going through a time when we're considering becoming engaged. And going through the process of writing this book has been very timely and given us a lot to think about. At this point, from a girl's perspective, there is something else I'd like to add to the discussion: Prince Charming. You know the guy I'm talking about. He's in all our favorite Disney movies. Every princess in distress had her Prince Charming who would come along just in the nick of time and rescue her from the wicked witch or evil ogre. And they would live happily ever after.

As I'm processing whether or not I'm personally ready for marriage and if "I would marry me," I must admit that most of my reservations are due to good ol' Prince Charming. All the Disney princesses were my dear friends growing up. They remain more nostalgically close to me than many other childhood memories, because they always had the ability to whisk me away into "happy land," where everything was ideal and nothing was boring.

Snow White was my favorite princess. She taught me many life lessons, like 1) it's good to have seven little men helping you out, and 2) the only way to have true happiness is through a prince.

I never thought that in a real relationship the expectations I borrowed from Snow White and all my beloved princesses would cause me to feel that something was missing. During the time we were first considering engagement, I often had a feeling of nervousness that seemed the opposite of how well we fit together. I'd think, *What's wrong with me!? Just relax, Danielle. Things will work out. But why do I get this strange feeling about being with Brent? What is it? Maybe it's this . . . or maybe it's that. Hmm, could it possibly be this?* I racked my brain trying to figure it out.

I dug up debris from past relationships and hurts, and found it personally helpful, but still not the ultimate answer to why I was afraid to move forward with Brent. I hated that things weren't going the way I wanted them to. Here was this guy I wanted to marry and felt I should marry, but there was this little thing underneath that I couldn't figure out.

Now I realize it was because of this: " . . . *the cheerful sound of birds singing and wedding bells ringing could be heard throughout the land as Prince Charming took the beautiful princess into his arms and kissed her.*" I wanted Brent to be my prince. I wanted him to make all my dreams come true. I wanted him to be perfect, my wedding to be perfect, and to live happily ever after. Notice the pattern? "I wanted." I had a selfish dream for a husband who would fulfill me.

This was quite a troubling realization. That feeling of nervousness was the fear that *if* Brent and I get married, he wouldn't be my prince. He wouldn't be perfect. All my dreams wouldn't come true. In fact, life may be a lot more the same than it will be different. I'll still be in the same boat—being a human in need of God. Brent will not complete a puzzle in me, nor will he be exciting and perfect every day.

I realize now that before I'm ready to get married, I need to come to the point where I don't expect Brent (or any guy) to complete a puzzle in me or to be exciting and perfect every day as a fairy-tale prince supposedly is. I need to be complete in myself and God before I'm ready to share my life with someone else.

DO YOU NEED TO SIT ON A DIVING BOARD?

Would you marry you? If you need to get your act together, do it before you get engaged. You will be better off, and one day, if you end up getting married, your marriage will reap the benefit of the relational health you bring into it.

Two

● ARE YOU ALL DATED OUT?

*T*risha made a big mistake. At least that's what she told her mom three months after her wedding. "I don't want to be married anymore. I want to be able to hang out with my friends and meet new guys. I feel like I made a big mistake marrying Rick, and now I'm stuck."

Big mistake? No kidding! How does something like that happen?

The last time I talked to Trisha was about six months before she married Rick. I had heard she was engaged, so I asked her about their relationship. She told me her dating relationship with Rick had been an on-again, off-again experience for a long time.

"Rick and I have been dating for five years, since I was a sophomore in high school. We've broken up three times, but every time after a few months apart, we always came back together."

"What was it that kept bringing you back together?" I asked.

"I'm not sure. I guess we just didn't see anyone better around and every time we got back together, we seemed to appreciate the other's qualities even more."

"That's great," I said. "So I heard you and Rick are engaged?"

Trisha hesitated as she answered, "Shortly after we got back together following our third breakup, Rick asked me if I would marry him. I said yes."

"Congratulations," I said. "So how are your wedding plans coming along?"

"Well," Trisha replied, "we've actually put our plans on hold. We've run into some yellow flags in our relationship and now we're trying to figure out if we're right for each other."

"I bet that must have been hard," I replied. "But if you're not sure, then you're doing the right thing to postpone your wedding. You're better off taking the time to be sure, or you could make a big mistake."

I'm not a prophet, but if the proverbial *famous last words* ever applied, this would be the time.

Not long after Trisha and I talked, I was surprised to hear that her wedding plans were back on. A date had been set within the next few months, and they were preparing for the wedding. I wish I could have had at least one more face-to-face conversation with Trisha before she got married, but that opportunity never came, since she was living in California and I was in Arizona.

In hindsight, if I could have had that conversation, I would have definitely asked her a few more questions. The two at the top of my list would have been, "Are you finished with any desire to date other guys?" and "Are you ready to make a one-man commitment to Rick for the rest of your life?" In my opinion, no one is ready to get engaged until both of those questions can be answered with a definite yes.

Now don't misunderstand me here. I don't think a person has to date a lot of people to find the right one. But if you are a person who enjoys the whole meeting . . . flirting . . . dating scene, then you need to make sure you've gotten that out of your system before you get engaged.

I'VE FOUND THE ONE

I've talked to a number of couples who got married after only one serious dating relationship—with each other. After they found each other, they never wanted to check anyone else out. That's Jacob's story.[1] As far as I can tell, Rachel was the first woman Jacob ever seriously set his eyes on and the only one he ultimately ever wanted to marry.

One day Jacob just *happened* to be hanging out at the Haran watering hole. For a lot of us, that would be like spending a refreshing afternoon at Starbucks. While he was there, in God's providence, Rachel just *happened* to bring her father's sheep to the same well at the same time. Sound familiar? "Yea, I just *happened* to be hanging out at Starbucks enjoying a grande decaf one-pump mocha when the girl of my dreams walked in. She ended up sitting at a table near mine. I said hi, and well . . . the rest is history."

When Rachel showed up at the well, she caught Jacob's eye. That, too, sounds familiar. Relationships often begin with physical attraction. The biblical account tells us that Rachel was "beautiful of form and face."[2] That's the Bible's discreet way of saying she was hot.

After Jacob saw her, he immediately stepped up and assisted Rachel in the labor-intensive task of watering the sheep. We're not told how long it took for the two of them to water the sheep, but we are told that Jacob kissed Rachel before he said good-bye. That certainly would suggest their first encounter turned out pretty well.

Actually, such a kiss in their culture meant nothing more than what a handshake or a hug would mean today. It was a sign of friendship and care. But nonetheless, the two of them must have hit it off romantically too, because a short month later, Jacob had a serious "I want to marry your daughter" conversation with Rachel's father, Laban. Even though Jacob had only known Rachel for a month, he was sure she was the one he wanted to marry.

To the average American, Jacob and Rachel's story then took an unfamiliar turn. Jacob offered to work the next seven years for Laban if he would allow Rachel to become his wife. Laban agreed to Jacob's offer. For seven years Jacob willingly worked for Laban, because he loved Rachel and wanted her to be his wife.[3] Seven years seems like an awfully long time to wait before getting married—but not for Jacob. His love for Rachel was so strong, and he was so sure that she was the right one, that the years of working and waiting flew by.

Those years didn't change his feelings for Rachel. His heart was still set on marrying her and her only, because she was the one love of his life. Finally the day came for Laban to give Rachel away to Jacob—but only after Jacob agreed to work *another* seven years for him on his farm!

"If that's what it takes, I'll do it." Once again, Jacob's actions proved the depth of his love for Rachel. He wasn't interested in checking out anyone else. He was committed to her and her alone and wanted her to be his wife for life.

I ONLY HAVE EYES FOR YOU

The singular love that Jacob had for Rachel is the kind of commitment it takes for a marriage to be successful. You must get to a point where you want no one else. You're finished with the single lifestyle. There isn't a lingering connection to anyone from your past. You're not excited about the prospect of meeting someone new in the future. No one else is on the radar. No one else is in your wedding picture.

If you get married before you're through dating other people, you will be susceptible to past and future dating dangers. You can be burned by an old flame or fall into a new fling. If you're not done with dating, you're not ready to get engaged or married.

Mark and Kim came to see that when a love triangle began to unravel their marriage. Everything changed when Suzy, a blast from Mark's past, resurfaced. Mark said he still loved Kim, but his past physical and emotional attachment to Suzy was pulling his once singular ten-year marital commitment apart.

"How did this happen?" I asked when they came into my office for help.

Kim jumped in. "After Mark reconnected with Suzy at their high school reunion, he wrote her an e-mail. At the time, he said he just wanted to send her some information that would help her sort out her spiritual questions."

Innocent enough, right? Perhaps, but the depth of his singular commitment to his wife and children was tested when Suzy wrote him back.

"Hi, Mark. Thank you for writing. I really appreciate your willingness to help me sort out the spiritual part of my life. I have really missed the relationship we shared. In fact, I've been thinking a lot lately about how I still care deeply for you and how I would love to see you again."

Several months after those two initial e-mails, Mark and Kim were still writing each other a few times each week. Innocent e-mails? Hardly. Mark was into an emotional affair with Suzy that was being carried on through e-mail and a cell phone Suzy had sent Mark to use for calling her.

"I would never have found out about his affair," Kim said, "if I hadn't seen an e-mail that Suzy sent Mark. I just happened to find it by mistake. What I read made me sick. Since I confronted Mark about it, things haven't been the same in our relationship."

"So Mark, what do you want to do?" I asked.

His words told it all. "I think I want to save my marriage, but I still have feelings for Suzy."

Mark and Kim were being burnt by an old flame that should have been put out for good years before. If that flame isn't extinguished, Mark and Kim will never experience marital intimacy—spiritually, emotionally, or physically. In God's marital arithmetic, two can become one, but not three.

If you have any flames from the past that are still lit, you're not ready to make a "one-man" or "one-woman" commitment. You need to put to rest any feelings that you may have for someone you dated in your past before you are ready to get engaged.

Looking ahead, there's also the possibility that you might meet someone in the future who will catch your eye, and you could find yourself thinking about how much fun the two of you could have together. Are you ready to give up the possibility of a relationship with someone you might meet in the future? If you're not, then you aren't ready to get engaged.

❯ BRENT

"Brent, do you want a girlfriend?"

I was asked the question while sitting in an office with old friends. They pointed toward the window. I peered outside to see a brunette more beautiful than the Los Angeles sky on a smog-free day (rare, but real pretty). Simon and Garfunkel started playing in my head, like in a movie, as I stuttered a response. "Uh, yes."

"We're serious. She works in our office," they quickly replied.

"Yeah. Sure," I minimally replied, hiding my excitement because guys aren't supposed to get excited.

A few minutes later Danielle and I were introduced. We timidly shook hands and said a quick hi, and then she turned and walked away.

My friends gave me her number and I courageously called a few days later, but she didn't answer. Of course I knew this was a strategic move on her part. *A smart girl,* I thought to myself. *That's good.* I left a mildly humorous message, hung up, and then waited nervously.

I turned on the television and began to watch *24.* It's one of those shows that ends with a cliff-hanger every week, and someone is always about to die or something is about to blow up— quite intense. I was an avid viewer. About three-quarters of the way through the show, I gripped a pillow, nervously wondering how Jack Bauer would get out of the death trap he was walking into, when suddenly—*ring-ring.*

She was calling me! In the middle of the most intense scene in the show! If I didn't watch, how would I know if Jack survived? How would I know if the bomb went off?

Ring-ring. I was confronted with two options:

1. Call her back later. *I could watch the rest of the show and then give this girl the proper attention she deserves,* I reasoned. After all, she didn't answer when I called before.
2. Answer the phone and assume Jack Bauer survives, because he's the main character.

Then I had a moment of clarity. I was actually thinking about the decision (TV or girl), because I was tired of playing "the game." I had dated lots of girls, and none of those worked out. Why would this be different? I was tired of dating, and because I was dated out, I decided I wouldn't answer. I turned to continue watching TV.

Ring-ring. The phone rang a third time and I began to ask myself how I would ever get married if I didn't date anymore. Would I ultimately want to choose TV over a girl? Of course not. I may be sick of dating, but I'm not stupid. I would answer the phone.

My hands were shaking as I pushed that scary green talk button, mustering a simple, "Hello?"

Danielle and I phone-flirted for hours that night. It was the beginning of this incredible relationship, and I was positive I would never tell her that I almost chose Jack Bauer over her first call. BTW, Jack survived, and he stopped the bomb.

COMPLETELY DONE DATING

Before you get engaged, be sure you date until your heart is content. Get it out of your system. If that means you need to date thirty people, then date thirty-one. Do whatever it takes to get to a point similar to the one at which Philip and Christine found themselves.

After Philip and Christine got engaged, they asked if I would help them with their premarital counseling and then perform their wedding. At our first premarital session, I asked my usual "So, tell me how you met?" question.

"We met at church," Christine said, "between services."

"Yeah, it was pretty cool," Philip added. "My brother introduced us, and we immediately hit it off. So I asked her for her phone number. Two days later I called her and asked if she'd like to go out."

I looked at Christine and asked, "When Philip called, what were you thinking?"

"I was glad he called, but I was also surprised. Perhaps shocked."

"What do you mean?" I asked.

Christine said, "I had just come off another dating relationship that ended badly. After that one ended, as far as I was concerned, I was done with dating guys. *Done*. In fact, just the week before, I had told God, "I never want to date another guy again."

"My story was similar," Philip added. "But for me I had gone for three years without dating. During that time I was just trying to get my life together and get past my past. I was content not to date. I'd had enough of that before. I was done with the single, dating lifestyle. I wanted the next girl I dated to be the one I married.

"Then I met Christine at church. That week I did something I never did. Usually when I got a girl's phone number, I would wait at least seven days to call because I didn't want it to seem like I was too interested. But this time I called after only two days. I couldn't wait."

"So, how do you feel now about dating others?" I asked.

"We're done with that," Christine replied.

Philip said, "The only person I want to date now and for the rest of my life is Christine."

I can identify with Philip and Christine. When I began dating Bernice, whom I have now been married to for thirty years, I was finished with dating. I'd had enough dates to know what kind of girl I was looking for or not looking for. As far as I was concerned, I was ready to settle down and was hoping my next dating relationship would be my last.

In every wedding ceremony I've performed, the bride and groom have given each other rings. Before they put the rings on each other's fingers, I like to encourage the couple to view these rings as visual symbols.

"As an endless circle," I say, "let these rings remind you of your unbreakable promise to be husband and wife for life. Let them remind you that your dating days are over. No more looking around. Let your love remain and always be singular . . . toward the one who gave you this ring."

If you're not ready to make that kind of commitment, then you're not ready to get engaged. If you still have feelings for someone from your past, you're not ready to get engaged. If you're still intrigued by the prospect of meeting someone new in the future, you're not ready to get engaged. Keep dating until you can say, *I only want to date one person from here on out.* And that person is the one you're thinking about getting engaged to—the one whose ring you want to wear the remainder of your life.

● BRENT

OK, this concept seems simple. I hear it and think, *Yes, I'm tired of dating. I've found the one I want to marry and don't want to look anywhere else.* But what does this really mean when it comes down to it?

How about this scenario: You walk into your favorite coffee shop, order that favorite drink, and sit down to journal or type away on a laptop. Gradually you begin to feel someone is watching you. You look up and what do you see?

An incredibly attractive girl (or guy) is checking you out. Not in a creepy way. In a very flattering and pleasant way. You smile back. You like the way he or she is sneaking glances at you. Innocent but flirtatious signals pass back and forth through the air between you. There is an immediate attraction, and you begin to wonder how magical the world might be if you ended up with this person. It's a delightful possibility.

Suddenly the individual gets up and comes over to sit next to you. Your heartbeat increases as you realize you have been holding your breath, and the song "So This Is Magic" pops into your head.

Once you're married, this scenario is only acceptable if the person you're flirting with across the room is your spouse! When married, all the other beautiful men and women are no longer options for you. You shouldn't even daydream about them. Are you ready for that? Am I ready for that?

For years I have played this game. It became a habit. I would see a pretty girl and look, wondering if she'd look back—wondering if something might happen between us. Granted, this usually ended with the girl just walking by, but still there was always that hope and fantasy of "what if" or "what would it be like?"

In thinking about this chapter, I came up with a basic question that is helping me figure out whether I'm really finished with looking for someone better: When I see a woman I am physically or emotionally attracted to, what do I do? Do I entertain the thought of being with her, or do I react as if my heart is already taken?

It gets harder when I take into account that once I'm married, I am supposed to answer this question the same way, even when things are rocky. Even when things haven't been going well or we're just not clicking that week. Am I willing to say that even then it won't matter if the girl at the coffee shop looks like a better option? There will be no other option. By choosing to get married, I am choosing to stop looking.

Three

● HOW DOES "TILL DEATH
DO US PART" SOUND?

*T*hat's it. No more dogs." We'd had our fill of dogs. We hated to admit it, but had to. We liked the *idea* of having a dog; we just didn't like actually having a dog.

At first we thought it was the dog's fault. After all, from the first day we got Kelly until we gave her away two months later, she was a pain to live with. The final straw came one night when the doorbell rang just after our family sat down to enjoy a spaghetti dinner. I don't remember why, but my wife, our three kids, and I all got up from the table to talk to whoever was at the door. In the few minutes we were away from the table, Kelly moved in. Actually, I should say on and in. Kelly found a way to climb up *on* the table, and then she dove *into* our plates of spaghetti. When we came back to finish our dinner, we found Kelly sitting in the corner of the room with spaghetti sauce all over her face. While she licked her chops, we fed our family that night at McDonald's and discussed her relocation plan.

We then decided we needed a dog that was already trained— to not eat spaghetti off our plates, among other things. Some friends who were moving asked us if we would like their very obedient golden retriever. We said yes.

For the first few days, our children did great with their "If we get a new dog, Dad, we will take care of it" commitments. But reality has a way of checking commitment. Our children's commitment died within the first week. Red would have died, too, if Mom and Dad hadn't stepped in. Then a few weeks after we got Red, our second son ended up in the hospital, possibly due in part to a dog-hair allergy. We found Red a new home.

You'd think we would have learned our lesson after two dog disasters, but not us. We still thought every family needed a dog, so we made a third attempt with Muffin. I'll spare you the Muffin Meltdown details, but the outcome was the same. One day about a month after Muffin came to live with us, she and Bernice went for a walk, and Muffin never came back.

We do like dogs. But we finally realized we just don't like the commitments required to raise one. That's why we've gone twenty years now without owning another dog.

COMMITMENT UP CLOSE AND PERSONAL

Of course a great marriage requires an even greater commitment than any of the commitments a family has to their dog. This lifelong unconditional marriage commitment is clearly defined in a wedding ceremony when the couple looks lovingly into each other's eyes and promises to be faithful for life. *For better or for worse, for richer or for poorer, in sickness and in health, to love and to cherish, till death do us part.* Now that's about as serious as commitments come.

If you're serious about getting married, you need to be seriously committed, in every good sense of the word. There's a difference between liking the idea of being married and actually being committed to living the life of a married person. I think somewhere along the way a light bulb has to turn on in your mind and clearly show you what you're getting into.

That moment came for the disciples one day when Jesus was confronted with a religious leader's sticky question about divorce. This person asked, "Is it legal for a man to divorce his wife for any reason?"[1] That question is still asked today. "When you get married, is there an escape clause? A loophole? A get-out-of-marriage-free pass?"

Jesus' pointed answer closed all the loopholes. After restating God's marital intention that "two become one," Jesus said, "Since they are no longer two but one, let no one *split apart* what God has joined together."[2] Separation by divorce, after marriage, isn't in God's plan. His plan is that *one couple* will experience *one marriage* for life. "Divorce for any reason?" Hardly! Even though Jesus did go on to say that adultery may lead to divorce, God never intended a marriage to end that way.

This was the moment the lights clicked on for Jesus' disciples. The seriousness of this lifelong marriage commitment led them to conclude that "it is better not to marry!"[3] Bingo. They got it. Jesus' message got through loud and clear. If you decide to marry, you're making a permanent commitment for life. Any commitment less than that compromises God's marriage design. If you can't make that kind of a commitment, you'd be better off remaining single. You'd think they would have already known that, but they didn't.

The disciples' world was pretty much like today's world. Divorce was rampant because, according to Jewish historian Josephus, divorce was permitted "for any reason."[4] The Talmudic writings of the rabbis said, "A bad wife is like leprosy to her husband. What is the remedy? Let him divorce her and be cured of his leprosy." Another rabbi added, "If a man has a bad wife, it is a religious duty to divorce her."[5] In the disciples' world, you could be labeled a "bad wife" for simply burning the bagels.

Talk about raising the bar to a place it had not been. Jesus wanted everyone to realize that marriage demands a high level of commitment—an unconditional covenant commitment where you totally and forever give yourself to another person for life. That level of commitment is almost foreign to people's thinking today, in any area of life.

IS TWO YEARS TOO LONG FOR YOU?

When it comes to signing on for any long-term commitment, we'd rather not. Take, for instance, the typical commitment to a two-year mobile phone contract. Even two years is way too long for most of us. But most of us will go ahead and sign on for two years because the phone and service offer that comes with a longer contract is too good to pass up.

"I got a great deal," we brag to our friends. And for a while it is. But then, not long after we're into our new contract, technology changes. Better phones hit the market. A friend shows us her "way cool" new phone that can do more things than we'd ever thought possible. Then we hear about another company that has better service—or a better deal. That's about all it takes and we're looking for a way out of our two-year contract commitment. We want to enjoy the best somewhere else. So we make the decision to cancel our service and get a better new phone for free by signing another two-year contract with another company, even if it means paying our current provider the contract cancellation penalty fees.

We are a culture that prefers short-term contracts and commitments on our own terms. If these agreements add to or protect our interests and benefits, wonderful. But when they hinder our right for happiness and life betterment, we want to be able to get out from under any and all contracts.

❍ BRENT

Beer goggles. Rumor has it that when you drink too much, you can get "beer goggles," or the loss of ability to properly discern what's in front of you. That's the rumor anyway. After being with Danielle for two weeks, I discovered something she and I now call "marriage goggles." Two weeks after Danielle and I started dating, we both began to sense that this relationship was headed toward marriage. We both just knew. And it was wonderful.

Our relationship was completely different from any we had been in. All my other relationships with girlfriends seemed forced compared to this. This one felt right. Whether she was right for me or not, these "marriage goggles" came on and started to impair my judgment. Too much too soon.

It became easy to say I would commit to Danielle. As weeks turned into months, our commitment grew as our relationship grew. *This is how it's supposed to happen,* I thought. Forever. For all time. And on and on with the one I love. For us, it was fun to think about getting married. Once we realized how we both felt, it became incredibly fun to imagine marrying each other.

When discussion of marriage begins, it automatically ups the commitment level several notches. For me this caused a problem: the line between how much I *thought I was committed* and how much I *should have been committed* so early in the relationship began to blur.

If I had read this chapter back then, I would have thought, *Danielle isn't like a cell phone contract. I want to marry her and be with her. I'm not going to leave. I know marriage is a commitment. I want to be committed. I want to spend my life with her, and I am going to commit accordingly.* But I had those goggles on (marriage, not beer).

Now, almost eighteen months into our relationship, I don't honestly know how much we should have been committed to each other back then. When I look around and see examples of bad commitments in society, it makes it hard for me to judge proper commitments. I thought I was ready to make a commitment—a good commitment—to Danielle. But as I later found out, my vision was impaired by those marriage goggles, and this got Danielle and me into a lot of trouble.

TODAY'S PREVAILING ATTITUDE

Writer and publisher Jeanne Belovitch pretty much captured the feeling of our time when she likened the contemporary attitude toward marriage to a child in a candy store. She said, "People are not trying as hard as they once did to keep a marriage together . . . they know there is a lot of candy out there."[6] If what you have isn't satisfying your sweet tooth, look for someone else. Move out and move on.

Prenuptial agreements represent just one of the many warning signs of a shaky marital commitment. A prenup is a premarital contract that states what property will be "mine" and what will be "yours" if a marriage is eventually dissolved by divorce. Call it what you want, a prenuptial agreement assumes the possibility of divorce, even before the marriage begins.

Failure is already a possibility. The "as long as we both shall live" vow is now often becoming "as long as we both shall love."[7]

Divorce lawyer Marvin M. Mitchelson worked on high-profile, big-money marital disputes involving scores of Hollywood stars. He once said, "I've never heard of a couple making a prenuptial agreement in which they didn't eventually get a divorce."[8] Veronica found that out firsthand. She and Jason set up a prenuptial agreement. Eight years into their marriage, they divorced. Sometime later she was asked if she thought prenuptials were a good idea. She replied, "I don't recommend them; it put up a divide in our relationship. It assumes things will go wrong."[9]

EVERY MARRIAGE REQUIRES COMMITMENT

If you get married, things are going to go wrong. After all, you are an imperfect person who is marrying another imperfect person. I promise you, you will get on each other's nerves. You will both do stupid things you regret. You will both say things you wish you could take back. You will both have days when you will say to yourself, *What was I thinking when I decided to get married?* But your undying, unconditional covenant commitment, "till death do us part," can outlast whatever challenges come your way. Are you ready to take on that kind of a commitment? That's the kind of commitment it's going to take to survive the challenges that are sure to come your way, if you get married.

Troy made that kind of a commitment to Jessica and later wrote, "The warm fuzzy 'feelings' of being in love are not going to last without a commitment to go along with them. In fact, there might even be days when I don't feel very loving. But that doesn't change the fact of the commitment I made when, in front of God and a bunch of friends and family members, I said

I'd have Jessica to be my wife. There were a lot of richer or poorer, better or worse, things said too, but in my mind the vows ended with 'I, Troy, take Jessica to be my wedded wife.' Period. No cop-outs, no prenuptial agreement bailout clauses, no 'for as long as we both shall love,' but 'as long as we both shall live.'"[10]

Ruth Graham, wife of spiritual giant Billy Graham, was once asked if she had ever considered divorce. She factiously said, "Divorce? No. Murder? Yes."[11] Of course, she is in no way endorsing murder, but she was definitely affirming her lifelong commitment to imperfect Billy. Ruth proved the depth of her "till death do us part" commitment to Billy for nearly sixty-four years.

Like Ruth Graham, I see marriage as a commitment for life. An absolute commitment to work through whatever challenges may come your way. For better, for worse, until death do you part. Is that a commitment you are ready and willing to make?

◉ BRENT

Though Danielle and I sensed marriage was up ahead after only two weeks of dating, we tried not to talk about it much. However, the mention of marriage sometimes just comes out when you're saying those cute, mushy things to each other. It's what you're thinking, and sometimes you accidentally vocalize a little too much.

Conversations about a possible future marriage gave Danielle and me a new sense of direction in our relationship. We began to make more decisions with our new endgame in mind. Our commitment level jumped up a few notches. Our love was nearly as good as the movies.

Eight months into our relationship, we were talking about marriage quite a bit but wanting to make sure we were being responsible and not getting ahead of ourselves. So we signed up for a "preengagement class" at church.

Unfortunately it turned out that "preengagement" was only in the class description and not in the actual class. It was a premarital class in which we mostly talked about how to be successfully married. But because we wanted to be smart, we stayed in the class. This led us from thinking about marriage occasionally to discussing it almost daily.

Our commitment took a big jump here. Things were getting very serious now. Marriage dates were being discussed. Ring sizes were taken. We even went to pick out rings. It felt as though there was no turning back, because we were already so far into the discussion. So we both adjusted our commitment levels—and our marriage goggles—and moved forward together.

Things gradually got more and more difficult for us. We'd bicker. We'd not have as much fun together. I'd say stupid things. She'd cry. I'd be distant. We'd both talk about how stressed we were. We discussed how nice our love would be once we were through this "difficult transition stage" of our relationship.

These difficulties kept escalating. We were praying about things and trying to be responsible and put God first, but for some reason things kept getting worse. It didn't make sense either, because we both had known we would get married eventually, as early as two weeks into our relationship. And we still felt that way.

And then one clear, crisp Sunday morning, we were walking to our premarriage class and just decided not to go. We would talk and pray instead.

It was on this day that we began to realize we were way ahead of ourselves, and the stress of it was tearing us apart. If we should have been at a commitment level 5, we were at a level 10. The weird thing is, we were trying to do it right. We went to a class. We prayed about it. We tried to follow what we felt God wanted. But in reality I think we let our dreams and marriage goggles get the best of us. We were too committed too soon, and it almost tore us apart.

Over the next few weeks, our relationship and commitment level began to painfully readjust. It was an awful time, full of hard conversations and several almost breakups. I thank God we got through it. And I thank God we didn't continue on the path we were going: marriage too early.

Now, in the interest of full disclosure, I'll ask Danielle about it too.

BRENT: Hi, Danielle.

DANIELLE: Hi, Brent.

BRENT: I'd like to thank you for joining me this evening to do this interview.

DANIELLE: Oh, it's my pleasure. Thanks for taking time out of your busy writing schedule to see me.

BRENT: Oh, thanks for noticing I did that. It's my pleasure to be here too.

DANIELLE: Yep. So what do you need?

BRENT: Is there anything you'd like to add about the marriage goggles?

DANIELLE: Yes, actually. Thank you for asking. I think the marriage goggles made it easy for me to avoid facing reality. I was so busy seeing things through the marriage goggles that I wasn't being honest about what I really felt. That is, that things weren't going well. I wasn't ready.

BRENT: Then how about our "time of adjustment"? Did I give a fair assessment?

DANIELLE: Yes, you did, from your perspective. But of course I saw it differently. Instead of thinking of it as a time when you'd say stupid things, I'd cry, you'd be distant, and we'd both talk about how stressed we were, I saw it as a time when I was avoiding how I was really feeling. I was scared to get into a permanent relationship and didn't really know what I was doing. I had made decisions so fast that I didn't know how to get out of them. I just didn't know what I was thinking. When I finally figured it out and let you know, I was so relieved. I allowed myself to feel how I really felt for the first time: confused and unaware of what was going to happen. So the "time of adjustment" was a nice time for me. I had bottled up all the energy for too long. However, I felt horrible that I had let you go on without my ever telling you. I didn't know if you were feeling the same way or not. So I was sad and worried over what you were thinking.

BRENT: So how does "till death do us part" sound now?

DANIELLE: Um . . . it feels weird. But maybe that's just because I've used it as a cynical phrase to correct others—often behind their backs—who I didn't think took marriage seriously. Because of this, a picture of God comes to mind where He's saying, "Till death do you part, Danielle! Till death do you part!" Honestly, I don't really know what it's like to commit to anything till "death," and so I'm a little afraid to trust that I'll do it. It makes me think I should judge people a little less when I get mad about their not being committed, and maybe think about myself. And Brent, you can't ask me that right now.

BRENT: Hey, hey. What makes you think I was going to? We have so many chapters left. Sheesh.

DANIELLE: Uh-huh. Right.

Through that readjustment time, Danielle and I drafted some basic rules for our new commitment level:

1. No discussing wedding dates or timelines whatsoever.
2. No discussing or looking at engagement rings.
3. No more premarital counseling. We dropped out of the class.
4. No more calling each other "fiancé." (Kidding. We hadn't been doing that. Even when we had our marriage goggles on, we knew that would have been too much.)

Now, almost six months after that readjustment, things are much better. We have learned how necessary it is not to force our commitment level. And we've learned about marriage goggles.

YOU ARE NOT YOUR PARENTS

Right now you may be thinking, *Yes, I want to make a lifelong commitment. No matter what's up ahead, I want to be with him/her for the rest of my life—for better, for worse . . . 'till death do us part. But—that's what my parents said when they got married, and they ended up getting a divorce. I'm so much like them in other ways, how do I know I won't end up doing the same thing?*

If this is an issue you are struggling with, I encourage you to read John Trent's book *Breaking the Divorce Cycle*. It's a great book that will help you work through these fears and will help you be ready to say, "Till death do us part."

The commitment you make when you get married will be *your* commitment, not your parents'. It will be a choice you make every day—to remain faithful to your promise to your spouse for life. You are not your parents. You can learn from their mistakes, but you are not destined to repeat them.

Four

● IS NOW THE RIGHT TIME OR NOT?

*O*nly a few very brave souls had the courage to get engaged during the two years I was at Westmont College. The majority of those in serious dating relationships, like me, waited until after graduation to get engaged. It's not that Westmont had a set of written rules that forbid engagement, it was more that no one wanted to put themselves at risk with the rest of the student body.

When I attended Westmont, the student body was small. We had fewer than one thousand students. That meant, like in a small town, everyone pretty much knew what was going on around the campus—especially on the rare occasions when someone got engaged. In the two years I was a student at

Westmont, I can remember only two or three guys who had the courage to do it. And each time, the news spread like wildfire to the entire student body. It became a topic of conversation from the dining commons to the dorms. But most of all, everyone waited with baited breath to see what would be done to the poor guy. That's right—*done to*!

Every groom-to-be, when he least expected it, was subjected to some form of public humiliation, thanks to his close friends. Within the Westmont culture there was an unwritten rule that said, "If you get engaged while you are a student here, you're going to get it." The *get it* took various forms. I can remember one guy who was stripped down to his underwear and tied to a wrought-iron fence. His friends then poured honey all over him and split open a feather pillow. They dumped the feathers all over his body, then pulled a nearby fire alarm. Of course, everyone poured out of the surrounding buildings and found this groom-to-be tied to the fence, looking like a half-dressed chicken.

On a different occasion, another recently engaged groom-to-be was kidnapped in the middle of the night and driven down the mountain from Westmont to a bird sanctuary five miles away, near the beach. Once there, his friends stripped him down to his underwear, threw him in the lake, and drove off. He was left to fend for himself and find a way to get back to the campus.

You can call me a coward or a chicken if you want. I look back and call it *smart*. I wasn't about to get engaged and be subjected to the engagement gauntlet. So my engagement didn't happen until three months after I graduated from Westmont. Partly because by that time I was far, far away from the engagement bruisers, but more due to what I believed was perfect timing.

They say timing is everything. That certainly applies to getting engaged. When I decided to ask Bernice to marry me, I considered it the second most important decision I would ever make. (The day I decided to become a Christ follower, by placing my faith in Jesus Christ for salvation, was and still is the most important decision I've ever made. I'd place my decision to get engaged second only to that.) Since marriage has huge lifetime ramifications, you need to be sure you're ready and that it's the right time.

Shortly after I graduated from Westmont, I knew I was ready to ask Bernice to marry me. There were four personal factors that assured me the timing was right. And now, after over thirty years of marriage and ministry, I can say from experience that these four factors are extremely important considerations in deciding if you're ready to get engaged.

Consider Your Personal Maturity

In the previous chapters, we looked at the importance of your personal readiness in character and commitment. Assuming you have a green light in those areas, let me now encourage you to consider your readiness in light of your age and maturity. Before you skip what I am about to say about your age, you need to know that I married Bernice at a very young age. She was only twenty-one and still in college. I was twenty-two and barely out of college. Getting married when you're young and in love can definitely work. I've not only seen that in our marriage, I've also seen many other couples who married at a young age and are still madly in love after many years of marriage. Being young isn't necessarily a red flag. It all depends.

Over the years, the average age of marriage has fluctuated up and down. In 1890, for a male it was a little over 26, and 22 for a female. Over the next sixty years, the average age gradually lowered to 22.8 for men and 20.3 for women. But after World War II, the age trend went back up again. By 1988, the average was 25.9 for men and 23.6 for women. Today it's reached its highest average age ever, with men around 27 and women at 25.[1]

As the statistics show, most couples are choosing to marry at a later age today than in previous years. That decision comes with both advantages and disadvantages. Marrying at a later age, according to marriage and family researchers Marcia and Tom Lasswell, can give you some definite advantages. They write, "Divorce rates are lowest for men and women who marry for the first time at age 28 or later."[2]

Psychologist Neil Warren has said that couples who marry around age 20 have an 80 to 85 percent chance of divorcing. He believes the correlation between an older age and fewer divorces is connected to a person's identity development. He writes:

> The theory goes like this: Young people can't select a marriage partner very effectively if they don't know themselves well. In this society, where adolescence often lasts until the middle 20s, identity formation is incomplete until individuals have emotionally separated from their parents and discovered the details of their own uniqueness. Prior to their mid-20s, young adults haven't defined their goals and needs. They haven't had time to learn to be independent. They aren't in a good position to know the kind of person with whom they could form a meaningful lifetime attachment. They simply need more life experience.[3]

As a general rule, marriage and family counselors have found that the older you are, the more likely you are to have developed healthy traits that will build a healthy marriage. That's why what we already talked about in chapter one is so important. Be the right person before you start thinking about marrying the right person.

But growing older does not guarantee growing up, any more than being young means a person is immature. I have known some very mature twenty-year-olds and some very immature twenty-seven-year-olds.

You may find it interesting to know that God's Word does not prescribe an ideal age for marriage. It does, however, suggest it was normative for couples to marry at a young age. Evidently throughout the years when the Bible was written, most people married somewhere between puberty and eighteen years of age.[4] Solomon himself suggested this when he wrote, "May your fountain be blessed, and may you rejoice in the wife *of your youth.*"[5]

The right age for marriage ultimately depends on whether or not you're growing up as you're growing older. Do you see signs of maturity? Wisdom? Unselfishness? Dependability? Godly character? Humility? As we get older, the chances increase that these qualities will characterize our lives. But you may be young and see them in your life now and in increasing measure. Whether you're young or old, you need to consider your readiness for marriage in light of your personal maturity.

Consider Your Financial Capability

When I was a still a college student, my financial portfolio was thin. I lived from paycheck to paycheck. I had no savings. All that I owned could easily fit into the backseat and trunk of my small car—a 1973 Capri. My on-campus jobs only paid me about $35 a week. My off-campus ministry position as the campus chaplain at Santa Barbara City College paid me an additional $250 a month. My limited income, after paying bills, left me at the end of each month with almost nothing to live on. But all of that changed soon after graduation.

Like every senior in college, I did *a lot* of praying and thinking about what I would be doing after graduation. I surely didn't want to go back and live with my parents after living away from home throughout my college years. I knew there was a strong possibility I could end up doing that if I didn't get a good-paying job.

That's why I was really excited when the church I grew up in called and asked if I would be interested in joining the full-time staff immediately after I graduated from college. I didn't have to think twice about that decision. That was a huge answer to prayer. Not only would my financial needs as a single person be met, but the starting salary would be enough to provide for Bernice and me if we were to get married. So I took the youth pastor position and started working at my home church two weeks after I graduated from college.

While I was in college, I knew I couldn't support a wife and go to school at the same time. Somewhere along the way, I learned this obvious fact: marriage requires money! At the very least, you as a couple need enough money to keep a roof over your heads and food on the table. Getting married and then living on the streets is not God's marital ideal.

Actually, God's words on this subject are rather candid: "If anyone does not provide for his relatives, and especially for his immediate family, he has denied the faith and is worse than an unbeliever."[6] The idea behind the words *provide for* suggests prior planning and thought. Marriage requires a financial commitment to do whatever it takes to provide for your family's needs. This passage suggests that even people who are not Christ followers understand that they are responsible to fulfill that kind of financial commitment. Not to do so would be inexcusable.

Since God invented marriage, He designed it to be a "leave and cleave" proposition. Leaving your parents physically is obvious, but the separation also needs to play out financially. The right timing for getting engaged must be considered in light of your ability to make ends meet financially. If you can't financially balance the books without help from your parents, you need to wait until you can.

Consider Your Time Limitations

Six hours on an airplane is way too long, unless you get wrapped up in a conversation that makes the time go quickly. Not long ago I had one of those riveting conversations with a twenty-something woman whom I sat next to on a flight from Frankfurt, Germany, to Atlanta, Georgia. Shortly after takeoff I found out that this newlywed wife, Lindsay, was flying back to the United States, where she was planning on getting a divorce.

Her husband, Mark, was in the military and stationed in Germany. After he completed his basic training in the United States, he and Lindsay got married while he was on leave. Shortly after they were married, Mark was ordered to Germany for an undisclosed amount of time. This meant that he and Lindsay began their new married life together in military housing in Germany. As it turned out, Lindsay spent almost all of her time at home alone.

She was pretty open with me about her marital frustrations. At one point, she candidly said, "The fact is, Mark is never home. He's married to the military, not me. It was a mistake for me to marry him. I think maybe it could have worked if he wasn't in the military. But now? No way! The timing of our marriage was all wrong. We should have waited, or never married."

Military service in the U.S.A. doesn't take into account Moses' instructions, which sensibly say, "When a man takes a new wife, he is not to go out with the army or be given any business or work duties. He gets one year off simply to be at home making his wife happy."[7] That's certainly what Lindsay wanted. She had expected a happy life together as a newly married couple. They needed time in the first year to build their new marriage and grow in intimacy as a couple. Of course that's impossible if you are hardly ever together or go without seeing each other for days at a time.

Many couples will tell you that the first year of marriage is the hardest. It's not surprising that more couples get divorced in the first year than any other year of marriage.[8] To prevent that from happening, God had Moses set up a first-year stay-at-home marriage mandate.

The best investment a couple can make during the first year of their marriage is a focused time investment in each other's lives. If a couple will choose to pay more attention to each other, and less attention to everything else, they will reap rich marital dividends now and in the years ahead.

If you're considering getting engaged and married in the near future, you would be wise to consider whether or not your current and projected time commitments will enable you to give your marriage the kind of focus it needs to get it off to a great start.

● BRENT

"I wish we had gotten married sooner. It would have been better to rush things. Taking our time was a big mistake."

I have never heard anyone say these things. None of my married friends would agree with these statements. However, I have had many friends say the opposite—wishing they had waited longer to get married.

Waiting to get married is not something we generally like to think about. We look forward to getting married because it means we have found the person we love and who loves us. We're committed to each other. We have a big celebration that's focused on us, and then we get to go on a honeymoon. It's almost as exciting as Christmas.

As I said in the last chapter, it was a real tough thing for Danielle and me to accept that our plans were rushed. It was hard to admit that something I'd been looking forward to for so long—something that was now within my grasp—needed to be put on hold a bit. But making the decision to take the marriage goggles off and wait until we were really ready was the second-best decision Danielle and I have made together. (The best decision was the one to be boyfriend and girlfriend and stuff.)

My relationship with Danielle has improved immensely since we readjusted. It has actually grown by leaps and bounds, because we have all this newfound freedom to get to know each other without the pressure of an impending marriage. I'm scared to think what would have happened if we had continued on that trajectory toward a rushed marriage.

So even though deep down we both still feel "marriage just might be in our future" (that's me choosing my words carefully), we found incredible peace in just taking a step back and enjoying the process of figuring it out. *Not* enjoying the process was a clear sign that it wasn't the right time, and it was a wonderfully freeing thing in our relationship to admit that.

Consider Your Sexual Control

Of the hundreds of couples I've worked with, every engaged couple has been "sexually challenged." And it's not because they didn't have an interest in sex. Actually, they had a lot of interest in sex, which is why they were sexually challenged. Most Christian couples want to "save themselves for marriage" but find it hard to wait.

God made sex for a couple to enjoy in marriage. But we all know keeping that standard is exceptionally hard, especially when you don't have the gift of celibacy.[9] If God did not give you the gift of singleness, you are going to struggle to keep yourself sexually pure. That being the case, Paul said it would be better for you "to marry than to burn with passion."[10] Fairly straightforward advice, isn't it? Can you imagine having a conversation about your sexual-restraint struggles with the apostle Paul?

JOHN: "Paul, I'm having a hard time saying no to sex before marriage. I want to control myself, but I'm going crazy. Amy just turns me on. I'm considering marrying her, but I'm just not sure. What should I do?"

PAUL: "Get married. As soon as possible!"

Instead of living a life of sexual compromise, God's plan is simple—get married. Don't start having sex. Don't start living together. Don't keep putting off getting married. Get married. Soon. If God has given you someone you could spend the rest of your life with, and you are sexually challenged, maybe it's a sign that you need to be thinking seriously about getting married. Soon.

Don't misunderstand what I am saying. I am not telling you to get married simply because you can't control yourself sexually. I am saying that your desire to share sexual intimacy may be one more sign, along with the others discussed in this chapter, that indicates the timing is right for you to move forward with marriage.

YOUR RIGHT TIME

When it comes to the right time, it's going to be different for everyone. Over the last three months, I've done weddings for three couples. The timing of these weddings was different for each one.

One couple is in their late twenties and very mature. He has an established career. She is a graduate student working on a master's degree.

The second couple is in their early twenties. Both have good jobs. One has graduated from college, and the other one will probably never go to college.

The third couple is nineteen and twenty years old. Really young. He was home-schooled and had always been ahead of the maturity curve. She grew up in a wonderful home that has given her a solid foundation for life and marriage. I can't say that they are fully mature, but I can say they are maturing. They are very teachable and very committed. They were even financially able to purchase a house to live in. When my twenty-one-year-old daughter saw their wedding, she said, "They are so young, but they just seem to be so right for each other and so much in love."

Ultimately, the right timing is something that you must decide. But you will do yourself a big favor if you make your decision in light of what you've read in the first section of this book. Are you personally ready to get married?

◗ DANIELLE

Once Brent and I put on those "marriage goggles," things started getting rocky. It became so easy to think he would ultimately fulfill me and to convince myself that this was OK. I stopped consulting God about my future "prince" (remember the Prince Charming syndrome?). I had found a wonderful and seemingly right candidate and was determined to see it work out. I figured he was the one who would resolve my past hardships and make all my dreams come true—including my agenda for what I was going to do with my life.

But something was missing. What was missing was something that should have been missing. It was designed to be missing. A man cannot replace God. The process I went through after this realization was uncomfortable and hard, but it was really important. It was something I needed to understand before I could know if I was ready to make a commitment for life to Brent. After coming to understand how the Prince Charming syndrome was affecting me, things began to improve tremendously, and now I'm enjoying the process so much! That sinking feeling, that stress—it's gone. But whenever I try to figure things out for myself, it comes back. I now see the necessity to trust in God and His timing while making sure I'm finding my fulfillment in Him and not looking for it in Brent. I've now come to realize that the solutions I formulate are nothing in comparison with God's plan. Being at rest with God's possibilities is peaceful.

This first section of the book has been great to help me take a look at myself and deal with some issues I need to figure out before I'm ready to get engaged and married. I don't think anymore that Brent and I need to become a perfect couple. I don't think we'll fulfill each other completely. And I also know there isn't a perfect Prince Charming out there anywhere. I'm learning to submit all of my dreams for my life to what God desires for me. I've had to learn to trust that even though God doesn't want me to live my own way, anything He has for me will be guided by His love and purpose for me. And I look forward to the day when I can say, "Till death do us part."

● BRENT

Getting engaged at the right time is going to be a wonderful thing. It will be something to praise God for and enjoy. I still hope and pray for it. The trick is just being honest about whether it's the right time.

It becomes difficult to discern what's right when fears get in the mix:

- What if we decide to slow things down, and then I lose her/him?
- What if something happens to one of us? I want to get married before I die.
- I don't want to end up alone. I want to get married and have all those worries behind me.
- I'm just tired of waiting. I want to get on with the "happily ever after."

These are the types of thoughts I was having when I was about to get engaged the first time. Now I realize I was trying to get what I wanted when I wanted it. Do you see God anywhere in the above statements? Me neither.

I'm convinced that the best way to start figuring out timing is through prayer. The process I went through to realize whether we should get engaged began with the prayer below. If you pray a prayer like this, submit, and expect an answer, God will work out the correct and beautiful timing. He'll make it clear.

Lord, thank You so much for my relationship with _____. I love her/him very much. You know that we're considering getting engaged and married. Please give me wisdom. If it's Your timing now, I ask that You would make that clear and help me to find peace in it. If it's not Your timing now, then God, I ask that You would correct that, that You would change our timing to be Your timing, that You would change our plans to be Your plans. Take away any selfish desires or dreams about marriage and replace them with Your plan, Lord. With this prayer I submit my engagement plans to You, God, and I ask that You help us as a couple to learn what it really means to submit. Thanks, Lord. Amen.

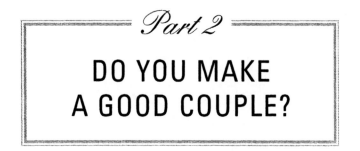

Part 2

DO YOU MAKE
A GOOD COUPLE?

Five

● ARE YOU "IN LOVE"?

*A*fter Andrew and Jen *fell in love*, they said they wanted to spend their lives together as husband and wife. But seven months after they met, Andrew and Jen decided they had *fallen out of love* and ended up going their separate ways. Their story began full of promise in front of 17.5 million people and ended with a separation announcement in front of millions more on *The Oprah Winfrey Show*.[1]

Andrew and Jen met on the third edition of *The Bachelor*, a reality television show. Twenty-six-year-old Jen was one of the twenty-five girls who vied for twenty-seven-year-old Andrew's heart. In the final episode of the season, Andrew affectionately looked into Jen's eyes and said, "Jen, I love you. I think that we fit perfectly together, and I look forward to a life of adventure, happiness, and family." Then he got down on one knee and placed an oval-shaped Harry Winston 2.8-carat diamond engagement ring on her finger and asked, "Jen, will you marry me?"

"Yes!" she answered. "Yes, I will."[2]

Afterwards when asked if they thought their love would lead to marriage, they said, "Yes, absolutely." Andrew said they were falling "more in love with each other every day." But four months later they parted and went their separate ways.

You can add Andrew's and Jen's names to the growing list of hopeful romantics who tried to find true, lasting love on a reality TV show. Not surprisingly, they instead found this to be reality: *falling in love* doesn't guarantee you'll *stay in love*. That's clearly obvious on reality TV. And it's also true in the everyday world of real life. Love that lasts requires more than simply falling in love.

Dr. Willard Harley focused on this in his insightful book *Fall in Love, Stay in Love*. Falling in love happens. Frequently. And it can be a wonderful experience. There's nothing like it. But staying in love requires something more. Much more.

HAVE YOU FALLEN IN LOVE?

If you're seriously thinking about getting engaged, you've probably fallen in love. Your experience could even be like what you've seen portrayed on television and in movies or heard in popular love songs.

In 1952, Doris Day sang a song telling the world that when she fell in love, it was going to be a love that would last forever. This famous love song continues to enjoy widespread popularity because it's what people long to experience—euphoric feeling that leads to a lasting love.

Sadly, that wasn't Doris Day's experience. She was married and divorced four times. Nat King Cole had a similar experience. His version of this song was released in 1956. It still is a favorite at weddings, but not even Nat fell in love forever. His first marriage didn't last. At his death, he was estranged from his second wife after having been accused of numerous affairs. Kenny Rogers, who also sang this song, has had an even worse experience, having now been married and divorced at least five times.

Falling in love and staying in love are two very different things.

● BRENT

Hmm, Doris Day? 1952?? It would be easy to say, "That may have been true back in the day, but things are different now."

But when I think about it, I bet it does still apply today. We constantly hear about celebrities and their relationships not working. And pretty much everyone I know has divorce somewhere in their family. Lots of marriages and relationships are failing. In fact, I have decided I like the term *failed marriage* better than *divorce*. Divorce sounds kind of distant or clinical and takes away the fact that there was a failure—a failure to do what needed to be done to avoid a divorce.

I used to have a working theory that every divorced couple would say they got a divorce because they "fell out of love." (I never really tested this hypothesis, but I think if this were fourth-grade science, I would get a good grade for the theory. It begins to fall apart, though, when you start asking questions. That's why I now refer to it in past tense.)

Is it even possible to fall out of love? I guess I fell out of love with past girls I dated. At least I thought I loved them. I really think I am in love with Danielle. But if we get married, how do I know I won't fall out of love with her someday? Or does the definition of *real love* actually make falling out of love impossible? (Hint—I've read ahead!)

ARE YOU REALLY IN LOVE?

Love often begins with feelings of infatuation, which actually may be nothing more than a biochemical reaction in the body. This chemical reaction can drive physical attraction and a psychological connection. It's often what was really happening when someone claims it was "love at first sight."

Scientists say that when you meet someone who catches your eye, your brain is flooded with phenylethylamine (PEA). Known as the "love molecule," PEA works in concert with dopamine and norepinephrine to trigger feelings of love.[3] The fact is, initial physical attraction between two people could have more to do with biology than love. That's why some say infatuation is *not* true love. Marriage and family therapist Pat Love says this about infatuation: "If I could make one change in how Western culture views relationships, I would change the perception that infatuation equals love. I have seen more heartache and disappointment come from this misperception than all others."[4]

Infatuation is short-lived. Its euphoric feelings typically last for only about six to eighteen months before they begin to wane (which, interestingly enough, is how long Andrew and Jen's love relationship lasted). Once the euphoric feelings wear off, you no longer find yourself constantly thinking about the other person. Your sweaty palms dry up. Your heartbeat goes back to normal. The butterflies in your stomach fly away.

When infatuation wears off, the true test of love begins. True love is more than just a feeling or something you fall in and out of.

LOOK BEFORE YOU LEAP

I like it when a pilot does a preflight inspection—especially when I am flying on that pilot's airplane. I'd rather be safe than sorry. I'd like him or her to look before we take the big leap. When first officers or captains do the preflight walk-around inspections, I hope they examine the plane closely. I want them to make sure no fuel, oil, or hydraulic fluids are leaking. They should check the fuselage and wings for cracks. Look at the wear and tear on the tires. Make sure the engines are free of all debris or blockage.

Several years ago an Aloha Airlines 737-200 plane managed to land safely after a major portion of the upper fuselage was ripped off at twenty-four thousand feet. Miraculously, of the ninety-five people on board, only one person died. Sixty-five of the remaining passengers and crew sustained various injuries.

After the frightening flight, one of the passengers told the accident investigators that when she boarded the plane she observed a crack in the fuselage of the airplane.[5] The crack was located in the section that ripped off during the flight. If only, right? If only she had reported what she saw to the airline ground personnel or flight crew before the flight. Maybe the death, injuries, trauma, and irreparable damage to the airplane could have all been avoided. If only.

Before you make the big leap and get married, you need to examine your love life closely. You need to do a careful pre-engagement love check. Your future welfare and happiness may depend upon what you see. I'd suggest you inspect the love you share from three different vantage points.

Check Out the Physical Side of Your Love

Of the three ways to look at love, this one will be the most obvious to see. Are you attracted to each other? Are you experiencing what the Greeks called *eros*—the love of physical attraction and sexual desire? Beauty may only be skin deep, but it nonetheless draws couples together.

Even if you think you're both ugly, which I doubt, there still needs to be something about the person you love that is attractive to you. Is it his personality? Her smile? Attitude? Disposition? Laugh? Voice? Something has to draw you to each other.

You say, "Well, that's so superficial and temporary." Yes, that's probably true. In fact, the older I get, the more I'd agree with that. I don't look like I used to look. My friends used to say when I was younger that I looked like the actor Omar Sharif (I think it was because our mustaches were similar). Now I won't tell you what they say about my looks. But my wife still thinks I'm cute. Gray hair and all. And she's still attracted to me.

The attraction kind of love is seen on several occasions in the Bible. The fact that Rachel was "beautiful in face and form" caught Jacob's eye. What caught his eye also caught his heart. The record goes on to say, "Jacob was in love with Rachel."[6] His was a love of physical and emotional desire. He longed to physically possess her and be in her presence.[7]

An even stronger biblical example of physical attraction and sexual desire is used to describe the love relationship of Solomon and the Shulamite woman. Prior to their marriage, she repeatedly longed for the day when she would enjoy his kisses.[8] She wanted to experience physical affection, which she in comparison saw as much better than wine.

Solomon responds by describing her appealing physical attributes. After commenting on her cheeks and neck, he summarizes his feelings with, "How beautiful you are, my darling! Oh, how beautiful! Your eyes are doves." She in turn replies by saying, "How handsome you are, my lover! Oh, how charming!"[9] Both were physically attracted to the other.

John and Michelle's story is like so many. Married since September 2005, they met when John came over to Michelle's house to fix a leaky shower. When John the plumber showed up at eight in the morning, Michelle wasn't looking her best. She later said, "He was really cute and he was my age."

After John fixed a small leak on Michelle's showerhead, Michelle said, "I called all my friends and said, 'Why did the cute plumber have to come over at 8 a.m., when I was looking horrible?'"

A few days later, Michelle's shower leak was back, so she called her home warranty company and asked them to send a different plumber who could fix the problem for good this time. But when the plumber showed up, it was John again. This time John found the real problem, and the two of them exchanged phone numbers. A year later they were married. Now Michelle advises single friends to break their shower, since you never know when a cute plumber will come through the door.[10]

I agree with Tommy Nelson, who said, "Attraction is both permissible and desirable. There is nothing wrong with being attracted to a person. If men were never attracted to women, or women to men, the human race wouldn't continue. Attraction, especially in our culture, is the first stage of any developing relationship."[11] The love of attraction will not only initially pull you together, it will make you want to stay that way for life.

⊙ BRENT

This is good news because I know Danielle and I are just going to get better and better looking, which I acknowledge will be hard, considering we're already topping out the hotness scale. (It's a 1–25 scale, in case you were wondering.)

OK, in all seriousness, this information about attraction is good to hear. Sometimes I feel as though our Christian culture tells us that it's not important. As if we're not allowed to talk about attraction, because we're just supposed to love our spouse unconditionally, no matter what he or she looks like. Yes, that's true, we are supposed to. But I think there's something to be said for physical attraction. It helps. Honestly. I'm just going to say it: it's easier to love someone you are attracted to.

As far as Danielle and I are concerned—no problem there. I'm definitely attracted to that girl!

Check Out the Emotional Side of Your Love

If you saw the original *Rocky* movie, you may remember the classic scene where Pauly was trying to understand why Rocky was interested in his homely sister, Adrian. In a conversation with Rocky, played by Sylvester Stallone, Pauly said, "I don't see it. What's the attraction?"

Rocky replied, "I don't know; fills gaps, I guess."

Pauly, still trying to understand, naively asked, "What gaps?"

To which Rocky reflectively said, "She's got gaps, I got gaps. Together we fill gaps."

Sure, it was just a movie, but Rocky made a good point. Adrian had empty places in her life. Rocky had empty places in his life. But when the two of them got together, they filled each other's gaps.

After God created man, He created woman because He said, "It is not good for the man to be alone."[12] God never intended for a man—or a woman—to try to do life alone. Each needs companionship. Close friends. The Greeks described this kind of love as *phileo*—the love of friendship, companionship, and emotional connection.

Solomon wisely said, "Two are better than one." Life is better when it's shared with a close companion.[13] Everyone needs someone who not only knows your name but also knows your heart and is committed to protecting it.

David and Jonathan shared that kind of friendship. The Bible says, "The soul of Jonathan was knit to the soul of David, and Jonathan loved him as himself."[14] Jonathan and David were soul mates, friends who shared *phileo* love. Nothing came between them. Not even Jonathan's father, King Saul, could tear them apart. They were inseparable. Each watched out for the other. When adversity came, they got through it together. Kindness and consideration prevailed in their friendship. They knew what the other was going through. When one of them needed encouragement, the other one hurried to give it. Their souls were connected through the experiences they shared and no doubt by the conversations they had. The heart of one was at home in the other's heart.

Even God the Father and God the Son share *phileo* love for each other. John writes, "For the Father loves the Son and shows him all he does."[15] The root word used here for love is *phileo*. Each is the other's friend. Theirs is a relationship of openness. Full disclosure. Complete transparency. Each knows what the other is thinking. Each knows what the other is doing. No hidden agendas. Each lives for the good of the other. What's on the heart of one is on the heart of the other.

Sociologists Steven L. Nock and Bradford Wilcox say that the biggest predictor of a woman's happiness in marriage is her husband's *emotional engagement*. In an interview with *Christianity Today*, they said this about a husband: "The extent to which he is affectionate, to which he is empathetic, to which he is basically tuned into his wife, this is the most important factor in predicting the wife's happiness."[16]

In their study "What's Love Got to Do with It?" Nock and Wilcox say the emotional attachment factor is of paramount importance. They report, "About two-thirds of all divorces in the United States are, at least officially, initiated by women. One of the key factors [they cite] is the emotional quality of their relationships."[17]

An emotional connection is of extreme importance. Without it, you will never share relational intimacy at the deepest levels. Now's the time to take a close look at the depth of the emotional intimacy you share as a couple. Are you experiencing *phileo* love? Are you soul mates? If you are, you will find yourself . . .

- eagerly looking forward to being together so you can share in each other's thoughts and activities;
- disclosing the secrets of your heart to each other;
- seeking the other's wisdom and advice;
- counting on each other's loyalty;
- giving each other a shoulder to cry on when life gets you down;
- seeking to understand the other's point of view, concerns, gripes, and desires; and
- enjoying fun times together as friends and companions.

Before you decide to get engaged and then married, you need to make sure you're best friends whose souls are knit together in love. The love of friendship ultimately will outlast the love of attraction.

Check Out the Sacrificial Side of Your Love

The Greeks also spoke of *agape* love—the love of sacrificial commitment. In order for a marriage to last, it must be grounded in agape love. Once again, now is the time to look closely at your relationship and see if there are evidences of sacrificial love. If it's there, you will be able to see it in action.

It's not hard to understand why this wife questioned whether her husband genuinely loved her and their kids when she wrote:

> I think the thing which hurts me the most (and he never sees this) is that he tells me he loves me all the time but has no idea how deeply I'm hurt when he comes home and shows no interest in our home. From the moment he arrives home, he is like one of the children . . . it never dawns on him that somebody has to take care of all this. So I feel like I'm nothing but a nag. How do I get across to my husband that his words and affectionate gestures mean virtually nothing when he . . . shows no interest in helping me?

Great question. "If he truly loves me, shouldn't it show in his actions?" The simple answer is yes! Words of love without sacrificial actions don't mean much. Genuine *agape* love will be backed up by servanthood. The Bible points to *agape* love as the most important way that a husband can love his wife. It says, "Husbands, love [*agape*] your wives, just as Christ loved the church and gave himself up for her."[18]

It's not hard to see how Christ loved the church, because it's evident in His sacrificial actions. Christ loved the church so much that He left heaven, came to earth, took on the form of a man, endured ridicule, rejection, and the abuse of people who spit on Him, beat Him, and then crowned Him with thorns and nailed Him to a cross, where he had a spear driven through His side. His death was the ultimate proof of the depth of His love. Jesus said, "Greater love has no one than this, that he lay down his life for his friends."[19] Christ loved His bride enough to make the ultimate sacrifice for her.

A great marriage is built on sacrificial love. Your commitment to sacrifice for each other now is an indicator of the degree you share this kind of love. What proof can you see right now that you are both ready and willing to put the other person above yourselves? Is it showing up in how you give of your time? How you do or don't spend your money? How you go out of your way to meet needs? Do you find yourself giving unexpected gifts? Do you help without being asked?

It's interesting that the Bible never tells a wife to love her husband through acts of sacrifice. This no doubt is due to the fact that she in comparison is more inclined to serve by nature. The biblical focus is instead on her attitude and demeanor. Her challenge will be to lovingly show Him respect.[20]

The single most important thing a wife can do to strengthen her marriage is to respect her husband by honoring him. *Agape* love is demonstrated when a wife treats her husband with a respectful attitude and honors him through respectful actions. So if you're a woman, you might ask yourself, "Do I demonstrate respect for this man who is in my life? Do I tear him down, or do I build him up? When we have a disagreement, do I express my opinion in a way that shows him I value him and am willing to resolve the conflict for the good of our relationship?"

◉ BRENT

(Begin Rant)

Somehow there is this idea that has permeated some parts of Christianity that says men are supposed to rule over women. That the man's being a leader translates into a wife's being the subservient slave. Or being inferior spiritually. I hate this—with a passion. I believe the Bible teaches that both spouses are equal. If you don't think so, then you're wrong. You can take my word for it, or just go read the Bible and figure it out for yourself.

Though this can go both ways. I had a roommate whose fiancée (eventually his wife) totally ruled over him. He was a puppet. This is not healthy, and it's definitely not biblical.

(End Rant)

Sorry for the rant. I just get worked up when I see people who are held down by the people who "love" them.

As a guy, I don't want a wife who just says, "Yes, dear. Whatever you say, dear." I want someone who will support and encourage me in my work and/or ministry. And I want to support and encourage her.

YOU NEED ALL THREE

Falling in love is not enough to give you a happy marriage. If you're going to marry one day, you need three kinds of love— the love of physical attraction, the love of emotional connection, and the love of spiritual action. Large amounts of *eros*, *phileo*, and *agape* will yield large amounts of real love.

Love is like a triangle. It has three sides: the physical, the emotional, and the spiritual. All three are necessary. The larger the triangle, the more love. A big triangle is good. A bigger triangle is better. You want to see your love triangle grow and keep growing. If you can see that happening in your relationship— fantastic! If you can't, then you need to step back and ask yourself, "Are we really in love, or is it something else that will wear off in six to eighteen months?"

◉ DANIELLE

The three kinds of love are really great to remember, just for the pure sanity of my mind. Thinking about them gives me a guide to go by and keeps me from worrying about some of my thoughts. Of course, God can help me with these areas, but sometimes I don't even know how to go with God without some sort of cognitive direction. It's always nice to realize the things you are thinking over are really real. Attraction, emotional connection, and spiritual commitment do matter. Actually, those have been the main things I have thought about when it comes to Brent and me. With this triangle of physical, emotional, and spiritual love, I can also see what areas are weak for me. Obviously, evaluating my relationship with Brent on a continual basis could be detrimental: I may wake up wondering, *Am I emotionally connected to Brent today?* when I really should just enjoy my time with him. But it's nice to be able to evaluate each area with a little more organization than usual—especially when thinking about getting engaged.

Six

● DO YOU COMMUNICATE EFFECTIVELY?

*O*ur two families were exact opposites when it came to communication styles. Bernice's family was quiet, reflective, soft-spoken, articulate, and considerate. Her dad, mother, two brothers, and sister didn't say a whole lot, but when they did speak, you knew it was going to be helpful. They practiced James's advice: "Everyone should be quick to listen, slow to speak and slow to become angry."[1] That was Bernice's family. They were careful to "not let any unwholesome talk come out of [their] mouths, but only what is helpful for building others up according to their needs, that it may benefit those who listen."[2]

My family, on the other hand, was just the opposite. We were loud, reactive, outspoken, verbose, and often inconsiderate. My dad, mom, two brothers, sister, and I said a whole lot. We were talking all the time—usually at the same time. Our unwritten motto was, *He who can talk the loudest, for the longest, has the best chance of being heard.* You didn't have to wonder what we were thinking. If we had something to say, we said it. The Gudgels' communication profile is found in the book of James, too, where he asks, "What causes fights and quarrels among you? Don't they come from your desires that battle within you?"[3] That was us—frequent loud verbal skirmishes, where each one of us fought for our personal rights.

The epitome of the differences in our family communication styles came out in our parents' responses to our engagement. After I asked Bernice to marry me, I felt I should ask her dad for his permission and support. I know what you're thinking: "Shouldn't you have asked him before you asked Bernice?" Yes, probably so. I have no idea why I didn't. I just didn't. So after I asked Bernice if she would marry me, and she said yes, we felt we should speak with our parents and get their permission before we proceeded with the engagement. So our first stop was Bernice's house.

After Bernice and I walked into the house and saw her parents in separate rooms, we decided we would each speak to one of them. She agreed to talk to her mother, and I would talk to her dad. I can still remember how my heart felt beating one hundred miles an hour when I walked into the family room, where Bernice's dad, Guido Ciminelli, was watching television. After I said, "Hi, Guido," I sat back and waited for an appropriate break in the program so I could tell him the good news.

After what seemed like forever, a commercial came on and I said, "Guido, I'd like to talk to you about something important."

"What did you have in mind?"

"Well, you know Bernice and I have dated now for three

years. Yesterday I asked her if she would marry me, and she said yes. Now I'd like to ask if you would give me permission to marry your daughter."

Guido responded like Guido always responded—without saying a thing. He looked at me and said nothing. Then, after what seemed an eternity, he thoughtfully asked one question: "Will she finish college?"

His question was understandable. He wanted to be sure that his and his wife's lifelong college dreams for their daughter, and Bernice's dreams for herself, would be fully realized. At that point, Bernice still had her junior and senior years of college to complete.

I quickly replied, "Absolutely. She will finish college while I work full-time."

Guido paused again and, after a few more moments of reflection, said, "OK, you may have my permission. I'm very happy for the two of you."

While I was speaking with Guido, Bernice spoke to her mom. Her mom's reaction was similar to Guido's. She softly replied, "That sounds great." Then she gave Bernice a hug and went off and cried.

I love the Ciminellis. They were everything I was not but hopefully one day would be. Under control. Thoughtful. Quiet. Affirming.

Next stop was my parents' home, where the reaction was the exact opposite. Fortunately, both my mom and dad were home and in the same room. After Bernice and I greeted my parents, I said, "Mom, Dad, I've got some good news. Yesterday I asked Bernice if she would marry me. She said yes. So we're engaged. Would you give us your support?" What happened next was typical Gudgel.

"Yes!!! . . . What?! . . . Finally!" followed by a million

questions and "suggestions." You would have thought our team scored a touchdown. Hugs and high fives broke out. It got loud in the room!

"We knew this was going to happen," Mom said. "This is great news. So, how soon will the wedding be? Come on, let's go someplace and celebrate!"

Two families. Two reactions. Both reactions were positive. Each set of parents were supportive and affirming in their own way. But talk about different.

Now fast-forward six months. Bernice and I had been married two months. If you had been close enough to our two families to know our different communication styles, and then come into our home, you would have thought you were watching the Gudgels and Ciminellis live under the same roof. We had perfectly brought into our marriage the two different styles of communication we had grown up with, which wasn't necessarily a good thing.

Here's how it was playing out. I was loud, Bernice was quiet. I was reactive, Bernice was reflective. I was outspoken, Bernice was soft-spoken. I was a talker, Bernice was a listener. I talked a lot, Bernice talked very little—in part, because either she couldn't get a word in edgewise or I just wasn't listening. It wasn't long before we realized something needed to change for us to experience healthy two-way communication.

Since those early days of marriage, a lot has changed. We've been married now for over thirty years. As you can imagine, we've learned a lot over those years about communicating with each other. We agree with the crowd that says healthy communication is absolutely essential for a great marriage. Without it couples are probably headed toward a train wreck. In fact, poor communication is one of the most common causes of divorce. That's why it's so important for you to carefully consider how healthy your communication is as a couple. This is an important determining factor in deciding to get engaged.

❯ BRENT

I used to think I was an excellent communicator. In fact, for the first year of Danielle's and my relationship, I thought we both were the best communicators ever. Only the first year, though.

You see, in college I was a communications major and took classes like Conflict Management, Interpersonal Communication, and Public Communication. Obviously (insert sarcasm here), since I am so educated in these matters, I am a master communicator.

Danielle is an English major. She loves to read books, she thinks her way through concepts and issues, and she is very good at expressing herself. If any couple should be good at communicating, it's us.

You may also be interested to know that Danielle is the one who talks a lot, and I am the one who internalizes and writes a lot. Through that first year, we were good at communicating. Then after almost exactly one year, we went through quite a bit of turmoil—one of those necessary times for growth after those chemicals in your brain (see chapter five) have worn off. Things were good with us, but there was something going on underneath that we couldn't put our finger on. We talked quite a bit about this transition but couldn't figure it out. We didn't imagine it would have to do with communication.

Brent and Danielle's Theory of Good Communication:

Talking a lot + Listening a lot = Good communication

We talked all the time. About deep things. About spiritual things. We felt we understood each other, and to think otherwise would be silly. Little did we know that we had become trapped in unhealthy communication styles.

Chances are, your style of communicating fits one of the following three profiles.

The Arrogant Boss

Have you ever worked for an arrogant boss? I have, and I hated it. He talked, I listened. He barked orders, I was expected to carry them out—without question or hesitation. He wasn't open to my suggestions, so I learned to keep them to myself.

You probably know someone like this. It could be a boss, a friend, or maybe a parent. Hopefully it's not the person you are dating or considering getting engaged to. If it is, that should be a definite yellow flag. You can spot arrogant boss types by their communication profile:

- They know better than you do—and they tell you so.
- They win, you lose.
- If they want your opinion, they'll ask for it—they've told you that too.
- Their motto could be, "Don't confuse me with the facts; my mind is made up."
- They might even say, "If you don't like it, don't let the door hit you on your way out."

The arrogant boss thinks he/she has all the answers and isn't really interested in what anyone else thinks.

This type of communication is one-way, top down, and domineering. This person usually comes across as autocratic, inflexible, demeaning, and often condescending. Solomon called this kind of person a fool. He said, "A fool finds no pleasure in understanding but delights in airing his own opinions."[4] Often this kind of person may even ask how you feel about something, but then, once you speak up, your thoughts and feelings will be dismissed. I know this by my own bad experiences with Bernice.

I hate to say it, but I've had too many conversations with Bernice where I asked her what she thought or what she would like to do, and then after she told me her ideas, I've ignored or dismissed them altogether. I know that's happened on more than one occasion, because she's told me so.

Here's one typical scenario from our past. See if you can identify. How do you decide where to go when you want to go out for dinner? Hopefully not like this:

"Why don't you pick where we go for dinner tonight, Bernice?"

"Are you sure?"

"Yeah, you pick a place."

"OK, how about . . . El Torito?"

"Oh . . . I don't think I should eat Mexican food tonight."

"OK, what about California Pizza Kitchen?"

"It's always so busy there. We'd probably have to wait half an hour to get a table."

"Well . . . where do *you* want to go?"

"How about Outback Steak House? That sounds good."

"OK, then let's go to Outback."

What do you call that kind of interaction? Dumb? Hopefully you don't call it typical. Hopefully it's not descriptive of your communication style. Basically, the other person is along for the ride as long as they are willing to go wherever you're driving.

That might work on a few occasions, but it will get old after a while. Because it's all about you: Your wants. Your desires. Your interests. Your rights. Your needs. Your beliefs. You, you, you!

In our marriage, we finally came to a night when I started

the same "Where should we go to dinner?" scenario again, and Bernice simply said, "I'm not going to pick, because we always end up going where you want anyway, so you might as well just tell me right now." That led to a long, overdue conversation about my communication style.

If it's all about me, me, me—me's got a problem. Maybe you've heard the old joke about the husband and wife who were married for fifty-plus years. On one occasion the husband was asked, "What's been the secret of your marital success?" He replied, "Two words. I always get the last two words in: 'Yes, dear.'"

Hopefully that's not you or the person you're considering marrying. One-way communication is the worst kind of communication. It's a red light that should bring you to a full stop, so you can consider how to move forward from here.

The Professional Counselor

The first time I went to a professional counselor, I was afraid someone would see me and think, *He's got a problem*. Of course I *did* have a problem. I just didn't want anyone to know. That's why the first time I went to see Dr. Rick Blackmon, I tried to sneak in without anyone seeing me.

I can remember as I walked toward his office, someone from the office next door came out and began to walk toward me. That's when I made a split-second decision and took an immediate left turn away from Rick's office. I actually walked in the other direction, because I didn't want that person, who I didn't even know, to think, *Oh, he's going to the shrink*. Yes, I needed help.

After my fourth attempt to get into Rick's office (just kidding), I finally made it into his waiting room. Rick and I had never met before. All he knew about me was that I was the senior pastor at a church nearby. All I knew about him was that he was a really good counselor and specialized in working with pastors.

When Rick called me into his office, our conversation began with his asking me the typical let-me-get-to-know-you questions. Then Rick got serious and said, "So Dave, why did you want to talk to me?"

"Well, I've got a problem." (Duh.)

"Yes, go on."

"Well, this is kind of hard for me," I said. "I've never had to talk to a professional counselor before. Whenever I've had a problem in the past, I've either been able to pray about it, work it out myself, or get some advice from a friend. But this time it's different."

"Go on."

"Well, OK. Here's my problem. Someone in the church I pastor has hurt me deeply, and I can't seem to get past the hurt. I've begun to have bitter feelings toward this person. I even get all tense and upset when I see a car that's like the car he drives! I've prayed about it and tried to get past this on my own, but I can't seem to let go of it. So I decided I needed to talk to someone like you to see if you could help me put this whole thing behind me and move on."

Rick was the right guy to talk to. God used him to help me get past that pain. He was able to pinpoint issues like justice and forgiveness and to help me see how to respond in a way that ultimately did me a lot of good and eventually even helped the person who had hurt me.

In the three sessions I had with Rick, I never got to know him as a person. He never talked to me about his family. He never told me about where he lived and what he did in his spare time. He never shared his hopes and dreams. He never shared his problems and shortcomings. That's the way a counselor/client relationship is supposed to be. Our relationship was good for me, but I couldn't say whether it was good for him or not (other than it improved his financial condition and he got satisfaction out of helping another person in need).

My relationship with Rick was not unlike what some couples share with each other:

- One person is the client; the other is the counselor.
- One has a need; the other has the answer to that need.
- One pours out his/her soul; the other stays emotionally detached.
- One is needy; the other is the caregiver.

Where the communication with an "arrogant boss" is basically one-way, this is more like one-and-a-half-way communication. One person talks openly; the other talks like a paid professional. It can even be sterile. Interaction is kept on a factual level. What the "professional" really feels and thinks inside—his or her true, innermost feelings and concerns—aren't revealed.

We all need advice. To seek it out from someone who is qualified to give it is a wise thing to do. Proverbs says, "The way of a fool seems right to him, but a wise man listens to advice."[5] It goes on to say, "Plans fail for lack of counsel, but with many advisers they succeed."[6] Our willingness to seek out and apply wise advice is smart. But in a relationship with someone you love and care about, you want it to be something more. In fact, you need it to be something more if you hope to experience relational intimacy.

Actually, Rick and I went on to enjoy a two-way communication relationship. After he fixed me up, he invited me to join his support group. That was a great experience for me. We met twice a month and it didn't cost me a thing.

In this care group I got to know Rick as a person, along with another marriage and family counselor and three other pastors. In the group Rick talked about his family, and I found out where he lived and what he did in his spare time. He shared his hopes and dreams. He revealed his problems and shortcomings. We met together for four years and became close friends who pretty much knew each other inside and out. We experienced genuine heart-to-heart two-way communication—the kind of communication that deep friendships are made of. This is the kind of communication that couples need—especially if they are serious about getting married.

The Indispensable Teammate

The best example I have seen of good communication is modeled by Bernice and her friend and coworker Cathy Morgan. Both work together as teammates directing the music and worship ministries at Bethany Bible Church in Phoenix, Arizona. Each has a vital role to play. Cathy is responsible for the music in the worship services; Bernice is responsible for the other details connected to programming the services. They are both very creative but see things from very different perspectives. They have often said, "Together we have one really great brain!"

Cathy and Bernice met over a cup of coffee. Right away, they clicked. They had perfect chemistry, in spite of their opposite personality styles. Cathy is a doer, a go-getter, a recruiter, and a "come on, gang, let's take that hill" leader. She wants to get it done right now. Big ideas just pour out of her. She wakes up early and goes to bed early. You always know what she is thinking or feeling, because she shows it on her face or will reveal it in her conversations as soon as it pops into her mind.

Bernice, on the other hand, is a thinker, an organizer, a coordinator, a connector, and a behind-the-scenes leader. When Cathy says, "Let's take that hill," Bernice figures out how they're going to do it. She sees what needs to be done to make the big ideas happen and happen well. She likes to get things done, but she's not driven to get everything done *now*. She is OK with leaving stuff on her desk and coming back to it at a later time. She stays up late and loves to sleep in. She'll gladly tell you what she's thinking or feeling, but only when she's thought it through and the time is appropriate.

Two people. Two different personalities. A great team on and off their field of play. Their hearts are knit together in love. Each knows what the other is thinking and feeling because they talk and talk and talk all the time. They know each other's strengths and weaknesses. They hold nothing back in their conversations.

When there's a problem, they get *everything* out on the table and deal with it. They call it "sharing the 10 percent." "Too often," they say, "people will talk about the safe and non-threatening 90 percent and ignore the dysfunctional or difficult 10 percent. But when the ten is ignored, conflict, mediocrity, and sin are left unresolved. Even when something is potentially touchy, we will openly talk about it."

Cathy and Bernice know firsthand the truth of Solomon's words, "Two are better than one, because they have a good return for their work."[7] They "carry each other's burdens, and in this way . . . fulfill the law of Christ."[8] They've learned when they are "speaking the truth in love,"[9] their relationship is better for it. They've also learned that when they "submit to one another,"[10] they end up with better results.

In the best marriages, the husband and wife communicate as indispensable teammates. Even if their personalities are very different, they learn to openly communicate with each other so that together they become much more than they would be alone.

● BRENT

I am a recovering "professional counselor."

Somewhere along the way in Danielle's and my relationship, I developed a pattern that whenever there was drama or conflict, I would listen and advise, while holding back some of my true feelings. This is not healthy. In those moments, I didn't want to share anything too deep or challenging about what I was feeling because I was scared it would be too much. I just wanted things to be peaceful. I didn't realize it at the time, but by doing that, I was keeping us away from some hard conversations that we probably needed to have.

What was confusing is that, as I shared earlier, we really were communicating a lot. We talked over things all the time. (From a guy's perspective, maybe even too much. Ha!) Then after that first year, we had a big "discussion" that resulted in my saying something stupid and Danielle replying with, "Just leave, Brent. Go home." Those words are never good in a dating relationship. Never.

Though a part of me really wanted to leave because the conversation was getting too hard (and I was a "professional counselor," remember), I didn't go. I stayed sitting there and we began to work through what was going on at the core. We had a long, overdue, hard conversation. We finally talked about the last 10 percent.

Suddenly everything was clear, and it made all the difference in the world. We had faked that small part of our feelings and held them back for a while, but ultimately they began eating away and eating away. When I finally got the nerve to share my last 10 percent, and she was able to share her last 10 percent—

not happy things to discuss—we realized they were necessary in the growth of our relationship.

Praise God we learned that lesson before getting engaged or married.

I thought my communication style was working toward a peaceful and stress-free relationship, but discovered that my playing the role of "professional counselor" was my way of avoiding hard but beneficial conversations. Necessary conversations. Worse yet, it didn't allow Danielle to get to know me as much as she deserved or was healthy. I was hiding the last 10 percent, hoping everything would just work out. But it wasn't working out, and Danielle was being put under unnecessary emotional turmoil because I was holding back.

Before that conversation, it was as though we had this very clean room with polished wood floors and a fluffy carpet. It looked great because we cleaned it often, but if you looked under the carpet, you would find a bunch of dust and crumbs on an unpolished part of the wood. And it just kept getting dirtier under there. The 90 percent looked great, but if we didn't get to that last 10 percent, then we weren't really taking care of the room.

Brent and Danielle's Corrected *Communication Theory:*

Talking + Listening + Last 10 percent = Good communication

Now I've learned that *talking a lot does not mean we have good communication,* even if it's about deep issues. *Communicating what's really going on does.* It has to include that last 10 percent.

YOUR COMMUNICATION STYLE

When I was in college, I read the book *Why Am I Afraid to Tell You Who I Am?* In his insightful book, John Powell writes, "All of us experience the human condition of fear and hiding. We all know something of what was meant by: 'But, if I tell you who I am, you may not like who I am, and that is all I have.'"[11] This natural fear is why Powell suggests that each of us tends to "act roles, wear masks, and play games."[12] Often these roles, masks, and games are used and played out in the levels on which we communicate with each other.

Powell characterizes conversation on five levels. The levels look like this, with Level 5 being the most closed, and Level 1 being the most open. I've added some simple phrases to help define each level:

Level 5   Cliché conversation—*What's up? How ya doin'?*

Level 4   Reporting the facts about others—*Did you hear about John and Laurie? They're engaged.*

Level 3   My ideas and judgments—*I think they're too young to get married.*

Level 2   My feelings (emotions, "gut level")—*I would never want to get married until after I've completed college and started a career. Probably not until I am at least twenty-five years old.*

Level 1   Peak communication—*I kind of feel the same way, but I also think some couples, like John and Laurie, may be ready for marriage at a young age. Yeah, you're probably right. I need to learn that not everyone needs to follow the same formula. Besides, we are young, and who knows how things might work out for us.*

This last level of communication, Level 1, is an absolute must for couples who want to have a good marriage. Both of them need to be able to express their true innermost beliefs and feelings. When their beliefs or feelings differ, they need to be able to express how they truly feel, openly and honestly, and still come out on the other side united and feeling affirmed. Each one has been heard, and both are still committed to each other as teammates.

You want to be able to share *all* of your heart with each other. Not just the part that the other person will like, but every part of you—what you think and what you feel. Then once you share these thoughts and feelings, you need to be able to work through your differences and find a solution that will put a win-win on the scoreboard. When that happens, you'll find yourself saying, "I feel valued and understood. I am so thankful that we are able to communicate with each other in a way in which each of us is built up and we arrive at solutions that are mutually satisfying."

If you were to rate your communication on a scale from one to ten, with ten being the absolute best, be aware that anything less than five is a yellow or red flag. Make sure you share healthy two-way communication before you decide to get engaged.

❯ DANIELLE

Reading this and thinking about the way I communicate was good for me. Actually, it was interesting that I could see myself in all of the types, depending on the situation. I'm finding I can change the way I talk to Brent by identifying which style I'm falling into at the moment. I'm also starting to recognize the triggers that cause me to slip into the unhealthy patterns. This is helping me understand myself better and helping me know how to become a better communicator. All of this insight is helping us become a better couple.

Seven

● ARE YOU ON THE SAME PAGE?

Since we don't have a dog, I'm the one who fetches the morning newspaper off our driveway. Once I get the paper inside, my daily ritual is pretty much the same. First I pull the paper out of the plastic bag. Then I sort the sections of the paper into three piles. The first stack is for me and usually contains the sports page, front page, and business section. Bernice likes to read the entertainment section, so the second pile for her is very small. The third pile is typically the largest. It contains the store and classified ads. This stack usually goes unread and ends up in the recycling can. We typically don't even look at the ads.

The first time I can remember reading classified ads was

shortly before I turned sixteen. Up to that point in time, I pretty much had no use for them, because I had nothing to sell and no money to buy what was being advertised. That all changed, however, once I got a job and had saved what I hoped would be enough money to buy my first car.

With three hundred dollars in my savings account, I started reading the classified ads every day, hoping to find a good car (I was a big dreamer). Within a few days I stumbled across an ad that read, "1963 Ford Falcon. Good condition. Nice paint and interior. Engine runs well. Only $300. Call (209) 555-5269." I thought, *Wow, this could be just what I'm looking for.* I quickly picked up the phone and called the number in the ad. After the owner convinced me that the car wasn't a wreck, I went over to see it.

As you can imagine, for three hundred dollars the car wasn't in pristine condition, but it did run. The interior wasn't bad. The radio worked. The body was free of dents. The tires were OK.

While the car had a number of good things going for it—like a bench seat—I can't say it had everything I hoped for. The engine was small, it ran slow, the stick shift was on the steering wheel (I would have preferred it on the floor), the car was painted puke green, and it didn't have air conditioning. It definitely had its issues. But for three hundred dollars, the upside (I could afford it, and it ran) outweighed the downside (not having a car and being stuck driving my parents' car). I bought the car.

For the next three years I did about everything you could to a car in need of some tender loving care. I rebuilt the engine, I had the interior reupholstered, I put new wide tires and rims on it, I had a loud stereo installed that broadcast my arrival when I drove up, and I had it repainted. Actually, my little Falcon became a fine car, and I enjoyed it for a while. But then

I decided to sell it. Cars are sold for a variety of reasons, and I had two. It was too old, and it didn't have air conditioning.

When I purchased that Falcon, I was living in Fresno, California, where the heat made the summers miserable. With an average summer temperature of 96 degrees, I hated driving around without air conditioning. So after three years of barely surviving the summer heat, I had finally had enough. Shortly after that, the classified ads once again became my daily friends. This time I both listed my Falcon for sale and began looking for a new used car that was no older than 1970 and had air conditioning.

My car ad read, "1963 Ford Falcon. Rebuilt engine. New interior and paint. Excellent tires. Superb stereo. Only $1000. Call (209) 439-7283." I was fortunate that within a few days time, someone saw my ad and came over and bought my car for my asking price. Not long after my car sold, I stumbled across an ad that read, "1971 Capri. Excellent condition. Original owner. Deluxe interior package including a sun roof and air conditioning. Asking $2400. Call (888) 226-9798." I ended up buying that car and enjoyed it for the next five years.

Classified ads are still a popular way to buy and sell cars. And now they have expanded beyond the printed page and moved into the cyberworld as well. Yet it still remains true, whether in the newspaper or on the Internet, they are a popular way to buy and sell just about anything.

They are also frequently used by individuals looking for a relational match. You know what I'm talking about: the personal ads. Similar to a car ad, every personal ad is descriptive. It tells you something about the person placing the ad:

SWF, 33, interior decorator, looking for new friends. Likes good books, adventures, travel, lively discussions. Works hard and enjoys being independent. Loves to laugh.

I'm a single mom, 37, who is an honest, good-hearted, loyal person. I'm intelligent and witty. I believe that we only have one life to live and I want to make sure when it's time for me to go, I have made a difference with my life. I'd love to connect with someone who shares the same aspirations. I'm looking for someone who doesn't have any current drama, very little past drama, and doesn't want any future drama.

SWM, 28, attorney. I am a very positive and highly motivated man who is intent on succeeding in both my personal and professional life. I am well on my way toward that goal and am looking for someone to share the journey with me. I travel with my career, so I don't have time for games. I like long walks on the beach.

Personal ads are descriptive. They tell you something about the person who wrote it (though many times they may simply tell you what people want you to *think* they are like). When the ad is sincere, it's often a direct line into the person's qualities, character, and values. This person hopes to connect with someone who is looking for similar qualities in a potential companion. Not only is this factor important among those looking for a new car, it's even more important for those considering making a commitment to each other for life.

❿ BRENT

Now I know what you're thinking:

What are these "newspapers" you speak of?

Well, newspapers are these things from the twentieth century that have personal ads as well as sports scores, TV schedules, and other articles of interest in them. They're kind of like the Internet but older.

OK, so what's a "personal ad"?

Glad you asked. MySpace is kind of like a modern personal ad. You describe who you are, who you want to meet, and what type of relationship you're looking for (casual dating, serious relationship, networking).

You know what I'm talking about. People write whole paragraphs about how they like obscure bands, have excellent taste, or would someday like to see a unicorn. MySpace is of course called "social networking," but it's really just a modern version of the old personal ads. We do it to advertise ourselves, even if we're not looking for someone.

When a blogger asked readers, "What is your secret to a happy marriage?" this was one of the many responses received:

> Love, respect, common life plans and values, honesty, trust, fun times together, sense of humor, sharing responsibilities, willingness to discuss relationship issues when they come up, sharing fears as well as successes, treating each other as equals . . . these all make our relationship strong . . . having some sort of hobby that you both enjoy doing together that gets you out of the daily grind can be wonderful bonding time . . . it could be cooking together, dancing, going to see live music, gardening, playing cards . . . whatever.[1]

The writer makes a good point. If you want a strong marriage, your values and interests need to connect on some level. The time to think about what that looks like in your life, and in someone you might hope to marry, is before you get engaged.

WHAT ARE YOU LOOKING FOR?

Recently I boarded a plane for a four-hour flight from Detroit to Phoenix. As it turned out, our flight left ninety minutes late. We sat on the plane at the gate for seventy-five minutes. After the plane finally left the terminal gate, we headed for de-icing. It was January in Detroit, Michigan, and the weather conditions were cold and icy, and snow was falling outside. Our pilot had no choice but to get the plane de-iced, which meant another thirty minutes before we could take off.

Prior to getting into the air, I had ninety minutes to get to know two single people sitting next to me. Neither Trish nor Carl knew each other, but both were on business trips to Phoenix. While we were waiting for our flight to begin, we introduced ourselves to each other. Then I sat back and watched Carl do his best to get Trish talking.

It was pretty obvious he was interested in her and just as obvious she wasn't interested in him. After Carl made a few attempts to get Trish to share more about herself, which she apparently had no desire to do, he pretty much gave up. It looked as if he was settling in for a nice, long nap, so before he could check out for the rest of the trip, I decided to ask them both a question.

From my aisle seat, I turned toward Carl, who was sitting in the middle seat, and Trish, who was sitting by the window, and said, "Would you guys mind if I asked you a question?"

Trish said, "I guess that would be OK." Carl added, "It depends. What did you have in mind?"

"Well, you're both single, aren't you?"

"Yes," they both said.

"I'm working on a book to help couples who are in a serious relationship decide if they should get engaged. I believe one of the important factors to consider is one's core values. So here's my question: If you were to one day get married, what values or character qualities would you look for in the other person?"

"Wow, that's a great question," Trish said. "I don't think I've ever given that much thought. But I'd say at the very least, honesty and humor."

"Yeah, I'd agree with those two," Carl said. (I'm assuming he really meant that and wasn't just trying to make points with Trish.) "I would also add loyalty and trust."

◉ BRENT

And then Carl and Trish looked at each other again (cue music), really seeing each other for the first time, and fell in love.

Kidding. The filmmaker in me can't help but think that if this were a Hollywood movie, that's what would have happened. Except they both would have been with other people who weren't good enough and would leave them for someone better—the person they just met on the airplane. Which is horrible, now that I think about it, because that's not what love is in the first place. We already went over that in a previous chapter.

Call them whatever you want—core values, key qualities, personal characteristics, likes or dislikes—they are essential factors in relational harmony and success. You need compatibility. It doesn't mean you have to be the same, or even agree about everything. But if you're going to spend the rest of your life with someone, you need to share the same basic values and motivations.

Amos made this point when he asked, "Can two walk together, unless they are agreed?"[2] The obvious answer is no. Unity and harmony depend on shared values and goals.

As God and the prophets were in prophetic alignment, you need to be on the same page with each other to some degree.

The bottom line of what is important to both of you needs to align. What that means and what that looks like is a matter of personal values preference. Do you know what core things are really important to you? Once you figure that out, you need to see if those things are also important to the person you are considering marrying.

ARE YOU A VALUES MATCH OR MISMATCH?

Every time people list or use a personal ad, or create a MySpace page, or enroll in an online matchmaking service, their personal profiles reveal what they perceive to be true about themselves. But the profiles also show what they hope to find in someone they might meet. When people are *looking*, they are looking for a person who has certain characteristics and who shares certain values. This was certainly the case with me when I met Debbie during my senior year in high school.

Debbie and I first met briefly at a Young Life meeting. A couple days later, I ran into her again during lunch at our school. Since both of us were on our way to the cafeteria, we decided to eat together. Our forty-five-minute lunch turned out to be a lot of fun and gave us both a desire to get together again. That worked out three days later when both of us attended a Friday night Young Life activity.

As Friday night approached, I can remember how excited I was to see Debbie again. I was eager to get to know her and thought for sure our relationship might turn out to be something special—perhaps even a boyfriend/girlfriend relationship. That night we had a lot of fun and seemed to have great chemistry. I found myself looking forward to seeing Debbie again, and the opportunity came two weeks later.

Debbie and I ended up on a thirty-hour bus trip to Dallas,

Texas, with eighty other students, which gave us the perfect opportunity to get to know each other really well. Over the course of our trip we talked about everything—our families, and likes, dislikes, dreams, convictions, and plans. Our time together on that trip gave us the opportunity to see each other at our best and at our worst. For thirty hours we had little sleep, no showers, and lots of junk food. I can remember one conversation in which Debbie was sharing her innermost feelings with me about something—and I fell asleep right in the middle of it.

After our bus trip to Dallas, Debbie and I pretty much went our separate ways. Our long conversations on the bus revealed we weren't on the same page in some key areas. We got along great, but found out we had a values mismatch. If I had written down some of our key findings, the list would have looked something like this:

VALUES MATCH:	VALUES MISMATCH:
• We both love God.	• She's very conservative. I'm not.
• We both love to talk.	
• We both value integrity.	• She's a strong Mennonite who holds to regimented practices. I have no interest in being Mennonite or holding to their practices.
• We both prefer having a few friends rather than a lot of friends.	
	• She wants a lot of kids. I don't.

A list like mine may or may not raise a relationship red flag. It really all depends on what values you consider negotiable and nonnegotiable. The big nonnegotiable between Debbie and me ended up being in the area of our faith practices. That issue helped us both realize our future would probably never be anything more than friendship. Looking back, that is exactly how our relationship played out. We became good friends, but nothing more.

WHAT ARE YOUR TOP TEN VALUES?

It's vital that you know what values or qualities you are looking for in someone with whom you hope to spend your life. You need to be intentional and discerning about this. There are some traits mentioned in the Bible that can quickly indicate red flags in intimate relationships:

Someone who does not share your *spiritual beliefs*:
"Do not be yoked together with unbelievers." (2 Cor. 6:14)

Someone who is a *gossip*:
"A gossip betrays a confidence; so avoid a man who talks too much." (Prov. 20:19)

Someone who has a *temper*:
"Do not make friends with a hot-tempered man, do not associate with one easily angered." (Prov. 22:24)

Someone who is *selfish*:
"Do not eat the food of a stingy man, do not crave his delicacies." (Prov. 23:6)

Someone who is a *drunkard or glutton*:
"Do not join those who drink too much wine or gorge themselves on meat." (Prov. 23:20)

Someone who is *sexually immoral*:
"I have written you in my letter not to associate with sexually immoral people." (1 Cor. 5:9)

The word *associate* in these verses suggests *partnership*. That makes a lot of sense in a business. If you align yourself with someone who doesn't share your values, you're headed for disaster. You can't sustain a partnership because you'll end up competing or going your separate ways.

Great companies hire employees who share their values. At Yahoo, that means an employee will embrace its six core values: excellence, teamwork, innovation, community, customer fixation, and fun.[3] It also means shunning things such as irrelevance, sloth, formality, status quo, same ol' same ol', arrogance, micromanaging, passing the buck, and wearing shoes at all times.[4]

It's God's intention that a married couple becomes one[5]— that they form an intimate partnership. To do this, they have to be on the same page in their core values.

So are you on the same page with each other? Not just in theory, but in practice? It's vitally important that the one you are thinking about spending the rest of your life with isn't just talking a good talk but is walking a good walk. There's a big difference between a paper value and a practicing value. You are what you practice more than what you say you practice. So for example, if caring for others is important to you, don't just ask, "Do you care about people? Because that's important to me." Instead, look at this person's life to see if he or she demonstrates a real concern for others.

What values are irreducible minimums in the one you hope to marry? What values would you call nonnegotiable, and which ones are negotiable? You really need to decide that.

If you need some help in thinking this through, use the following list to help you get started. In fact, I'd suggest you circle the qualities or values that are most important to you. Then define them as either nonnegotiable (these must be there) or negotiable (would be nice to have, but not absolutely necessary). Then circle your top ten and ask yourself how these are playing out in your life right now and in the life of the person you are considering marrying.

Faith in God	Honesty	Fun
Exercise	Humor	Integrity
Loyalty	Staying out of debt	Family focused
Having pets	Church attendance	Saving
Moral standards	Risk and adventure	Reading
Giving	Activity	Traveling
Healthy eating	Respect	Friendships
Staying at home	Decisive	Gratitude
Listening	Talking	Serving
Kindness	Unselfishness	Trust
Transparency	Hospitality	Optimism
Ecology	Truthfulness	Discipline
Tolerance	Character	Balance
Alcohol	Change	Having money
Patience	Frugality	Marital roles
Routine	Surprises	Sports
The arts	Working at home	Social activities
Cleanliness	Accountability	Conservative dress
Innovation	Entertainment	A clean house
Good manners	Acceptance	Faithfulness

I found myself admiring Suzy's wisdom when I heard her story. She and Chad had been dating for a long time, and everyone assumed they would be getting engaged and then married. But when it became obvious that he was going to be proposing soon, Suzy decided she had to break off the relationship before it went any further.

When I asked her why she did that, she said, "I came to

realize that if I married Chad, I would end up resenting him because the kind of life he wants is so different from what I want. He lives a very traditional, ordered life, but my life is very nontraditional. I love variety and change and adventure. Chad wants stability, sameness, predictability. I realized that God created us with different values and passions. And once I realized that, I knew I couldn't marry him."

Three years after Chad and Suzy broke up, God brought Todd into her life. They met on a matchmaking Web site. Each at the same time had decided that even though it was a long shot, they would try posting on a relationship-finding Web site because it offered a one-week free trial membership. If they didn't meet anyone after a week, they'd just cancel.

Soon after their trial periods began, they found each other on the site. Todd and Suzy lived on opposite sides of the country, but what they saw in each other's profiles seemed compatible, so they began getting to know each other through that site until their trial memberships expired. Then they continued through e-mails, instant messaging, and eventually phone calls. One thing led to another. They met, dated, and now are engaged to be married.

"This time," Suzy said, "it's completely different from how it was with Chad. Todd and I are on the same page. He values what I value. He embraces what I embrace. We complement each other perfectly. I am so glad I woke up to the importance of shared values. That was a huge ah-ha moment for me. I used to think that as long as two people love each other and are both believers, that would be enough. Now I'm so glad I didn't settle for that. God had something so much better waiting out there for me."

Suzy's right. Your dreams and aspirations, at some level, need to match or at least be going in the same direction. Your core values need to align with each other. Whatever you do, don't get engaged with the unrealistic hope that one day this person's values or lifestyle will change. Don't even begin to count on that happening. If you can't marry a person for who he or she is now (and may very well be for the next fifty years), don't get engaged. This potential life partner may never change. Can you live with that?

❍ BRENT

On my first date with Danielle, I tried to scare her off. I tried to prove we had different core values.

Some backstory: Before meeting Danielle, I had been in a few relationships where we got along wonderfully, but at the core there were some basic differences that contributed to the relationships not lasting. Believe me, I had tried to make them work, but in the end, our forcing of the relationships just caused more hardship. Because of this, by the time I met Danielle, I had a better understanding of some core values I would need to find in a spouse. The short list looked something like this:

1. A heart for missions and justice issues.
2. Supportive of and excited about my film work.
3. Willingness to travel and live overseas, as well as in the United States. Wherever God wants, basically.
4. Being OK with my not having steady or secure work as I follow where God leads. (My profession is a series of freelance jobs.)

Over the past few years I learned that it wasn't easy to find someone who met all these "requirements." In fact, for a time it seemed virtually impossible. Then I went out with Danielle.

You know how when you go out with someone for the first time, you often try to put on a good face so they will want to spend more time with you? Well, on our first date, I kind of did the opposite. During a pre-dinner conversation over tea, we both chatted and chatted with youthful exuberance, until suddenly we just stared at each other in silence. We had hit a metaphorical wall and were stunned, because all of our core values were lining up—perfectly.

We both had the exact same passions. We had similar goals for our lives. Our priorities and views on money, church, and service were completely compatible. These were things I had never found compatible with anyone I was attracted to. The more we talked, the more we realized how in line our core values were. This was something we weren't prepared for.

After the first fifteen minutes of that date, I think I knew that this was a girl I could marry. I was scared and confused. *There's no way things can be going this well,* I reasoned. The only thing I could think to do was prove we weren't actually as compatible as it seemed. That was it! I brought out the big guns—the more controversial topics, such as whether job security is biblical or if women should be in church leadership. Yet we even had similar views on those. My adrenaline started pumping faster as the reality of the situation sunk in. I must not have been thinking completely clearly, because I decided to bring up the most controversial core value I could think of: diamond rings.

I sneakily opened with, "I found out the craziest thing this week. A friend and I were researching diamond rings, and did you know that the tradition of giving a diamond ring was actually created through an ad campaign in the forties and fifties? They even advertised that you should spend three months' salary on it to prove your love!" I kid you not. This is true, and it's really what I said to Danielle.

"Really? That's incredible." Her eyes instantly lit up with passion as she began to rant, "I actually don't ever want a diamond ring. I think it's horrible that even if they're supposedly 'conflict free,' diamonds are still coming from slave labor. Plus, they are basically not even rare, except for the fact that a few companies hoard them in order to raise the value and fabricate an unnatural desire. I don't think I could ever be with someone who wanted a diamond ring. It's what they represent, you know?"

It was as though she was reading my mind. I was sitting across from a beautiful girl whose core values were compatible with mine. Not the sugar-coated version, the actual deep version.

Suddenly, I realized that all those past relationships where our values didn't align were forced. I might have thought we were on the same page because we both believed in God and wanted to serve Him, but underneath, things didn't actually fit. We were fooling ourselves.

This relationship was different. There was nothing forced about it.

◉ DANIELLE

Thankfully, before I met Brent I really understood that I had to align my values with whomever I dated. That's actually what allowed me to move forward so easily with him. Obviously, there have been other things to work through, but knowing that our core values aligned really worked out some of the kinks at the beginning. I'm glad Brent and I meticulously analyzed this area of our relationship. It has really worked out with our long-term goals. We don't have to debate over whether our goals align or our core values are the same. And we don't have to worry about any future bitterness because these core values aren't being lived out, which I think is a problem for many couples.

Eight

● ARE YOU SPIRITUALLY CONNECTED?

When I was growing up, my parents frequently argued over which church our family would attend on Sundays. When my dad won the argument, we went to the Baptist church. When Mom prevailed, we went to the Methodist church. For years my parents fought tooth-and-nail over whose religion would be our family's religion.

Dad was raised Baptist. The Baptist roots go deep in the Gudgel family tree. One of my uncles used to claim an ancestral connection to John—the first Baptist!

Dad, along with his four brothers and three sisters, was raised in the First Baptist Church of Chowchilla, California. It's where Mama and Papa (that's what we called my grandparents) had each of their eight children dedicated as infants. Later each was baptized at that church, and eventually, most of them were married there. In recent years, it's become the place where our family funerals have been held. Dad says, "As we were growing up, every time the church doors opened, we were there. Sunday morning, Sunday night, and Wednesday night—we faithfully attended." You could say my dad's B+ blood type stands for Baptist.

Mom, on the other hand, was raised Methodist. Although the Beebes weren't as faithful in going to church as the Gudgels, they nonetheless took their religion seriously.

Mom was baptized a Methodist, grew up attending Sunday school at the Fresno Methodist Church, and was married in the church she grew up in. Whenever we grandchildren stayed at our grandparents' house over a weekend, we were taken to the Methodist church on Sunday. As far as Mom was concerned, being a Methodist was the only way to go. She wanted us, her kids, to be Methodists too.

For over eight years my parents fought over whose church would be our church. Neither wanted to give up their religious upbringing. Their arguments typically broke out on Saturday night and often lasted right up to the last minute on Sunday morning—just before we left to go to church.

I hated listening to them fight about which church to go to on any given Sunday. Even at a young age, their arguments seemed contrary to how a person who goes to church should act. Their faith didn't seem to work for them. I used to think, *If this is what religion does to a person, I'd rather have nothing to do with it.*

My dad finally said, "Let's agree to alternate churches every other Sunday. One week we will go to the Methodist church and the next week we will go to the Baptist church. That way we can keep everybody happy. How does that sound?"

Mom said, "Well, I'd rather take the kids every week to my

church, but I guess if you don't want to become a Methodist, and since I don't want to be a Baptist, this will have to do. I think your solution will be better than fighting every week over whose church to attend."

Amen to that, I thought. I had heard enough of their arguing about church. In fact, at that point I would have been happy if they never brought the subject up again.

Have I said enough for you to get a clue? You can spare yourself and your future family a lot of unnecessary pain by making sure you and the person you marry are on the same page spiritually. My parents learned that very important lesson the hard way, first through their bad experiences, but eventually through some good experiences.

My parents' lives took a turn for the better one Friday night when my dad told us kids to get in the car, because he was taking the entire family to a Lay Institute for Christ. We told him we would rather just *lay* around the house, but he replied, "No, we're going to church tonight, all day tomorrow, and all day Sunday. So get up, get ready, and get in the car."

Spending an entire weekend at church wasn't my idea of fun. But it was God's way of dramatically changing our home. What my parents heard at that conference completely changed their lives. Both Mom and Dad made personal decisions to completely surrender their lives to God through Jesus Christ.

Shortly after that, I began to see positive changes in my parents. One of the obvious ones came when Mom joined Dad's church, and the First Baptist Church in Merced, California, became our family's church of choice.

What a difference that made in our home! We began to pray together as a family, and their newfound faith started to make a difference in their personal lives and their marriage. Not long after their decision, I, too, made a faith decision, following their footsteps and placing my faith in Jesus Christ for salvation. When a home is united in faith, it can have a life-changing impact.

As in my parents' case, even though a couple may share the same overall spiritual beliefs—they may both call themselves Christians—there can still be significant differences in their values and practices. As a couple, you need to take the time to talk through those things to see if you are both on the same page.

YOUR SPIRITUAL CONNECTION MATTERS

I firmly believe the spiritual dimension in marriage is indispensable. It has the power to change lives and homes, especially when both husband and wife share similar spiritual beliefs and practices.

It's not by mistake that when Paul wrote about selecting a prospective spouse, the one thing he chose to focus on was the spiritual connection. Paul clearly said that a follower of Christ must marry another follower of Christ. As he described it, the other person "must belong to the Lord."[1]

Having been raised in a home where I saw firsthand the effects of spiritual disharmony, even between two professing Christians, I am in complete agreement with Paul. If you want to do yourself a big favor, make sure you and the person you marry are on the same page spiritually. If you're a follower of Christ, marry another follower of Christ. Otherwise, your life and your home will suffer from your differing spiritual beliefs.

Often when a believer marries an unbeliever, there is a detrimental impact on the believer's faith. Moses acknowledged this potential danger when he told the Israelites not to marry someone who did not share their spiritual beliefs. Before the Israelites returned to the Promised Land, which was occupied by people who had substituted their own man-made gods for the one true God, Moses warned them, "Do not intermarry with them. Do not give your daughters to their sons or take their daughters for your sons, for they will turn your sons away from following me to serve other gods."[2]

Unfortunately, they ended up doing the very thing Moses told them not to do. The Israelites "took their daughters in marriage and gave their own daughters to their sons, and served their gods. The Israelites did evil in the eyes of the LORD; they forgot the LORD their God and served the Baals and the Asherahs."[3]

A sad picture, isn't it? I'm sure those parents had the best of intentions when they gave their kids away in marriage. They probably wanted their children to experience the joys of companionship, child rearing, security, and love in marriage. But you have to ask yourself, was the trade-off they made worth it? Sure, they ended up married, but they also ended up abandoning God. I call that a bad deal.

After God took a backseat in their lives, these newly married couples were left to make their marriages work in their own strength. Let me tell you, that's a shaky way to begin and grow a marriage. The Bible goes so far as to say, "Unless the LORD builds the house, its builders labor in vain."[4] Trying to build a home without God's help is destined for trouble and failure. I doubt that's what you want out of marriage!

STAY OUT OF A SPIRITUAL MISMATCH

Years after Moses warned the Israelites not to intermarry, the apostle Paul gave similar advice in his two letters to the Christians in Corinth. In his first letter he told them to marry only a fellow believer. In his second letter he added, "Do not be yoked together with unbelievers."[5]

Since most of us don't use yokes today, we miss the full

impact of what Paul is saying. In Paul's day, a yoke was a bar or piece of wood that linked two animals together. When two working animals, like oxen, were evenly connected by a yoke, it empowered them to do more together than they could have done apart. But if the animals were unequally yoked, in kind or size, the work was hampered by their differences. Everything they would attempt to do together would end up being more difficult.

Paul urged Christ followers not to be yoked together with an unbeliever. The differences are too great. Doing so would make it difficult or impossible to work and live together. A spiritual mismatch would make it tough to be married.

I not only saw that firsthand in my own childhood, but I've seen it many times since, as I've counseled spouses who are in a spiritual mismatch. Stephanie's story is pretty typical.

> I know I should have never married him. I knew what the Bible said about marrying an unbeliever, but I ignored it. I just figured it would all work out. Well, it hasn't. I am so frustrated. It's gotten to the point in our marriage now where he doesn't want me to go to church on Sunday. He says it's the only day we can have together as a family. But I want our two children to grow up in the church. I want them to continue going to Sunday school. I can't imagine them not being able to enjoy seeing their friends and teachers at church and benefiting by all that they are learning. So, Pastor Dave, what should I do?

You know what I tell wives and husbands who come into my office frustrated by their spouse's lack of spiritual interest— or worse yet, their desire for no one else in the family to be involved in a church? I basically say, "Work for a compromise. That's all you can do right now. Let him/her know how you feel, but don't ram your opinion down his/her throat. Accept whatever she decides. Be kind and loving and patient. Do your best to show Christianity through your love and lifestyle. And pray like mad that God will change his/her heart."

I'd like to say that advice always works, but it doesn't. If you're reading this book because you're thinking about getting engaged, the best thing I can say to you is don't make a spiritual mismatch mistake. If the person you are considering marrying is not on the same page with you spiritually, back off.

DISCONNECTED BY SPIRITUAL DIFFERENCES

This was of such great concern to the apostle Paul, he went on to ask the Corinthians five penetrating questions. He said, "What do righteousness and wickedness have in common? Or what fellowship can light have with darkness? What harmony is there between Christ and Belial? What does a believer have in common with an unbeliever? What agreement is there between the temple of God and idols?"[6] For Paul, the only appropriate answer to those five questions was *nothing* or *none*, due to:

- *Identity differences.* One has been declared righteous by God; the other stands before God as unrighteous. One has the Holy Spirit living in them; the other does not. Both pursue a lifestyle that fits their inherent makeup.
- *Citizenship differences.* One is a child of the kingdom of God; the other is a child of the kingdom of this world. As members of opposing kingdoms, each is at war with the other at some level.
- *Authority differences.* One is a follower of Christ; the other doesn't acknowledge His authority. Each looks to a different authority for marching orders.

- *Faith differences.* One believes Christ is the only way to salvation; the other rejects Christ's salvation offer. Each sees the path to eternal life differently.
- *Worship differences.* One worships the God who made the world; the other worships the world's self-made gods. Each sees the purpose of life differently.

The bottom line? It's not a good idea to marry someone who does not share your spiritual beliefs, even if you are on the same page in a number of other common areas such as values and interests. Without shared spiritual beliefs, you are setting yourself up for future problems. Strong marriages are built on shared spiritual beliefs.

I like to think of a couple considering marriage as two distinct circles. Each one has his or her own spiritual beliefs. In marriage, two people seek to become one. What each spiritually believes and practices will either pull them together or push them apart.

As the two diagrams below show, couples who view life through a similar spiritual lens experience greater connection (see Diagram 1). More spiritual harmony equals more marital intimacy. But couples who have little or nothing in common spiritually will never experience intimacy to its fullest degree (see Diagram 2).

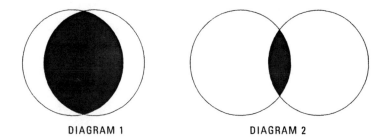

DIAGRAM 1   DIAGRAM 2

BUILD THE SPIRITUAL FIRST

I hate to say it, but it's true. Most couples ignore the importance of the spiritual connection. It's not that they don't give it any thought. They do, but often not until they are engaged and are making plans for the wedding. Then they come to see someone like me and ask for spiritual help.

It's as though they want God's blessing on their marriage and feel the best way to derive this benefit is by getting married in a church. So after a couple finds the perfect church that fits their wedding plans, they make an appointment to see the pastor. Whatever spiritual benefit they may derive often comes down to the pastor's counseling, prayers, and words spoken in the wedding ceremony.

Let me ask you to consider how the spiritual dimension has played out in your relationship to date. Which of the following two diagrams fits you? Which comes first, the physical or the spiritual? What is the foundation in your relationship?

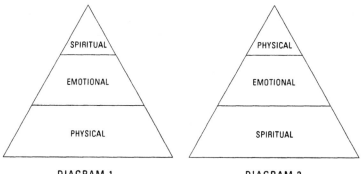

If you dating experiences have been more like Diagram 1, you're in the majority. This is the progression most couples take. First, they are attracted to each other physically. Then they get physically involved to varying degrees. Today that usually includes sex before marriage.

If this has been your relational path, there is a good chance your emotional and spiritual dimensions are underdeveloped or neglected. It may be that the primary way you experience intimacy is through the physical. If this is the case, when passion is high, intimacy feels high. But when the physical wanes, you may find yourself asking, "What is it that we really share as a couple? Is it physical only, or do we really have something more that we can build a strong marriage on?"

Diagram 2, on the other hand, is descriptive of a couple who has taken the time to develop the spiritual dimension in their relationship first. They know this area is essential for a strong relationship and ultimately is foundational in a strong marriage.

As Diagram 3 pictures, with shared spiritual beliefs and practices, a couple will find themselves growing closer to each other as they grow closer to God. Oneness with God leads to greater oneness as a couple. With God's help, they will also grow in emotional intimacy. Their hearts will become one. And by waiting for marriage to have sex, they will find themselves expanding their spiritual and emotional connection.

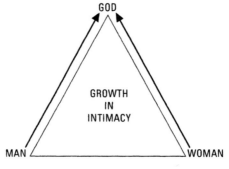

DIAGRAM 3

DETERMINE YOUR SPIRITUAL CONNECTION

So what's the bottom line of what I am saying? Simply this: *A strong spiritual connection is essential for building a strong marriage.* Consider the following three aspects of your spiritual life to help you begin to get a read on this area of your relationship:

- *Spiritual beliefs.* Are your spiritual beliefs in agreement on essential doctrines of the faith? A few vital areas to consider could include: God, Christ, the Holy Spirit, the Bible, sin, salvation, baptism, spiritual gifts, the resurrection of Christ, Jesus' second coming, heaven, and hell.
- *Spiritual commitments.* Have you both made a commitment to follow Jesus Christ as Lord and Savior? Look at the following commitment continuum. Are you both at the same place in your spiritual commitments? If not, what will this mean in your relationship and in your spiritual practices?

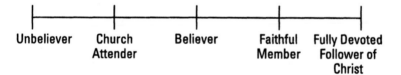

| Unbeliever | Church Attender | Believer | Faithful Member | Fully Devoted Follower of Christ |

- *Spiritual practices.* Here you need to consider such matters as: worship, prayer, ministry involvement, moral decisions (drinking, smoking, lying, media intake, etc.), giving tithes and offerings, witnessing, and church involvement.

Discussing the issues listed above can be very helpful in sorting out what is going on in your lives spiritually. If my parents had considered these issues before they were engaged, they would have realized they were on very different pages spiritually, even though they were both "Christians." Looking at them may not have thrown up a red flag—perhaps a shade of yellow—but it would have been better for them to have worked that out before they got married. This way they could have found a solution that would have drawn them together spiritually, instead of allowing their differences to push them apart for so many years.

IT'S A DIFFERENCE MAKER OR BREAKER

Bernice and I met at the church both of us were attending with our families. This church gave us similar spiritual beliefs and practices. At the time when we began to seriously date, we were also each seriously committed to the Lord.

Our relationship pretty much began through the spiritual dimension. We prayed together and studied the Bible together. We worshiped together on Sundays. We ministered together at the church through our choir and youth-group commitments. We went to summer camps and winter retreats together. When it looked as though we might be headed toward engagement, we went to a local Christian bookstore and purchased a couple's Bible study on relationships. Every week we set aside time to talk about what we were learning from this study and what it meant to us individually and as a couple. Both of us took seriously the spiritual dimension in our relationship with God and each other. Without hesitation I can say we, and now the family we have raised, are better for it.

While you are considering getting engaged, you need to decide what place, if any, the spiritual dimension will have in your relationship. Of course as I've said, I believe it needs to be at the center of your lives. A vital relationship with God is essential to experiencing all that marriage can be. Whatever you decide, you will be better off if you're both on the same page spiritually in your beliefs, commitments, and practices.

● BRENT

Oh no! Danielle and I come from different Christian traditions.

If you are reading this and come from a different background from the one person you love, it does not necessarily spell disaster. It's just going to be a bit harder at first, and you're going to have some hard conversations. But chances are that, as Danielle and I figured out along the way, you already know it'll be harder.

One of the first things that attracted Danielle and me to each other was our spiritual . . . vigor, if you will. We were very compatible. Yet, though we are both Christians, we come from different religious traditions.

Danielle grew up in the Free Methodist church. I was born nondenominational. (Literally, I came out of the womb a nondenominational.) Before meeting Danielle, I didn't even know what a Free Methodist was. It was more confusing to me than anything: *method* implies structure and *free* is the opposite of structure. Thus began my prayers for Danielle to convert to nondenominationalism. (OK, I didn't really pray that. Danielle actually came from a very strong tradition. And in case you're wondering, yes, they do believe in and love God.)

There are a lot of differences in how our current faiths have been shaped by our past spiritual experiences. Danielle grew up in contact with dozens of other churches across Southern California because of her denomination. I kind of just grew up with my own church. I went to a summer camp with a bunch of other random kids from random churches, while Danielle went to a camp for Free Methodist pastors' kids (called PK Camp—no, I am not making this up).

Danielle and I both have a plethora of positive and negative experiences that are a result of our upbringing in the church. Our past experiences affect how we presently define our spirituality, yet our present beliefs are what are important. For Danielle and me, it just has taken a bit of time to work through the differences to get to similar ground.

Believe me, because of our backgrounds, we had a lot of redefining to do, to make sure we were on the same page. It was not fun, but it was incredibly necessary. We found that even though we could go to the same church and worship together, it was important to dig deeper to see where we were defining things differently. And then once we addressed those issues, we could decide where we agreed and where it was OK to disagree.

I have two closing thoughts for this chapter:

1. I think it's OK for a couple to agree on Christ but come from different styles of worship, as long as they can agree on a unified faith and where to worship, and as long as their kids aren't confused.

2 If you think you agree on everything spiritually, try this one: "Darling, what do you think about women in church leadership?" I'm convinced it's a good conversation to have. And maybe you'll be like us, where both parties agree at the core and just end up arguing over semantics.

● DANIELLE

Brent and I have discussed spirituality a lot because of our dual experience as pastors' kids. We both often critically analyze the church and talk about what we think about it. We may even have more preferences and quirks than most, which isn't necessarily a good thing, it's just how it is. This, therefore, is a very good reminder that we still have to take note of practical questions like, what church would I ideally want to raise my children in, and are we able to pray and study together?

Nine

● ARE YOU BETTER TOGETHER THAN APART?

Thirty years ago I faced a dating decision that I sensed could impact the rest of my life. Looking back, I can honestly say it has.

The decision came during my senior year in college. At the time, I was a student at Westmont College, but I was away from the Santa Barbara campus for a semester. For four months I, along with thirty other sociology students from Westmont, was living and taking classes in San Francisco.

We were in an urban studies program. Our curriculum included classes taught by Westmont professors, but the program's primary focus was on practical experiences in the city. My thinking was radically changed by my dropout prevention internship assignment and the downright frightening city life experiences that made up the program. The police car ride-alongs and being dropped off to live on the streets of San Francisco for three days with only a dollar in my pocket changed me. It also made me wonder if I would ever see Bernice again.

My dating relationship with Bernice had begun in earnest two years prior to my San Francisco experience. Bernice and I knew each other because we attended the same church and high school. After a couple of false starts, our casual friendship turned into a serious dating relationship while Bernice was a senior in high school and I was a sophomore in college.

Through a series of what I would call divine circumstances, we both ended up attending Westmont. Our dating relationship continued to grow while we enjoyed our first year on the picturesque Santa Barbara campus. But now my enrollment in the Westmont urban studies program meant I would be living five hundred miles away from Bernice for the next four months.

Four months is a long time to be away from someone with whom you've had a two-year dating relationship. The time and distance alone will show you what you have or don't have as a couple. It will also test your commitment. It did mine—especially after Cindy and I became friends.

Cindy was one of my classmates in Westmont's urban studies program. She and I ended up getting to know each other pretty well, partly because we were paired together on several class projects and assignments. But then we, along with some of the other students, also started to hang out together. Over the next four months, our casual relationship turned into a close friendship.

I can remember having long conversations with Cindy about our dreams and desires. We played tennis and board games together. We learned to juggle together. We had fun together in the city. From trolley car rides to Sunday services at various churches, we shared many enjoyable experiences.

Then it hit me. I was faced with a choice. Bernice and I were still dating. She still considered me her boyfriend, and I still considered her my girlfriend. So what did that make Cindy? I was at a crossroads. Would my relationship with Cindy continue as a friendship, or would I pursue something more? Was I ready to give up my dating relationship with Bernice and seek more than a friendship with Cindy?

It took awhile for me to sort out my conflicted feelings and thoughts. I wanted to be sure that whatever happened, I didn't make a foolish decision that I would later regret. I can remember spending a significant amount of time praying and asking God for wisdom and focusing on the ways our lives could complement each other.

Well, since I've been married to Bernice for the last thirty years, what I ultimately concluded is obvious. I realized that Bernice and I together could make an incredible couple. Our strengths and differences complemented each other perfectly. Once this realization came into focus, I made a singular commitment to keep dating Bernice with the thought that one day we might get married.

WHEN DIFFERENT IS GOOD

The idea of a couple marrying because they complement each other isn't an insignificant sidelight. It's an essential consideration and legitimate reason for marriage. In fact, it's at the heart of why God created a man and woman to enjoy life together.

From the beginning of time, God said, "It is not good for the man to be alone."[1] So God created a man and woman to complement each other—in body, soul, and spirit. Man needed "a helper."² Together they could *do more* and *be more* than they would have if they had lived life alone. Their differences and similarities would mold them each into better people.

As I look at my life today and through the past thirty years, it's obvious I've needed a "helper." Just ask my kids and colleagues. My life has been so much better than it would have been had Bernice not been my wife. To this day, I know I owe most of my accomplishments in the home, work, and community to God's incredible work through Bernice and the many ways she has complemented my life. (She just leaned over my shoulder and said that I've complemented her life too.)

◉ BRENT

This is true. I can affirm that my parents complement each other greatly.

This chapter of course brings up a question I should probably ask: Are there places in my life where I need someone else to help me be better and more capable? The answer is obviously no; I've pretty much got everything figured out. Kidding. There are numerous areas in my life where I know I need help. I am reminded of them often.

At this point in my life, I've done enough work and ministry to realize that I am not capable of doing everything in the entire world, as I want to believe I am. Actually, I think it's common for all of us to go through a time in our life when we think we know everything. I like to refer to this stage of life as "college." When I would visit my parents while in college, I'd spout off all this new stuff I'd learned and things I wanted to do. It was an incredibly exciting time, and I think part of a natural progression toward adulthood. For some, this behavior happens earlier or later than college. Unfortunately, for some, this stage lasts their entire lives.

Now, a few years after college, I can see in hindsight that it

could have been dangerous to make an important relational decision (i.e., engagement or marriage) while thinking I knew it all. I
very easily could have married the wrong person because I was
unaware of my weaknesses that needed complementing. The
decision back then would have been based more on how much
fun we had together. Now I'm focusing more on how well we
complement each other.

Through many failures, I eventually learned the hard way that
I have many weaknesses, and now that I see these weaknesses,
it is rather exciting to see someone come into my life who can
help offset some of them. Whether it's related to something
simple like my social skills, or something more complex like how
I make decisions, I definitely want to be with someone who can
help me where I'm helpless. I think that's one of the great things
about good relationships.

When I work with couples who are considering marriage, I
encourage them to think about the ways their similarities and
differences could add to or subtract from their relationship.
Here are a few areas you may want to consider:

- How are you similar and different in your
  personalities? In your perspectives?
- What, if any, activities and interests do you share
  in common?
- Do you like the same types of food?
- Are you introverts or extroverts, or a combination
  of both?
- How does each of you handle conflict?
- How many children were in the homes each of you
  came from? What does this mean in your relationship?
- How do you handle money?

Let's take just two of these areas and see how understanding these kinds of differences and similarities can be an asset in a couple's relationship.

PERSONALITY DIFFERENCES

My friend John Trent likens the primary personality types to four animals: a lion, an otter, a golden retriever, and a beaver. "Charge" is a lion's watchword. If you are a lion, "taking charge" and "charging ahead" aptly describe you. Otters are fun-loving, spontaneous, and carefree. They are the life of a party. The golden retriever describes a friendly "how can I please you?" personality. A beaver epitomizes organization and detail. Its motto is "a place for everything and everything in its place."[3]

I like to think of myself as a gentle lion. (Yes, it is possible.) Bernice, however, is a fairly balanced combination of all the animals. If the two of us were lions, I doubt we would have ever married. My guess is conflict would have prevailed and pushed us apart. But her balanced personality has toned me down and helped balance out my natural "let's take the hill right now" personality. I used to run people over, but God's work through Bernice has taught me much about working with people in healthy, nondemeaning ways.

One of the very first things I do with a couple who is looking toward marriage is to give them a personality survey. It's incredible how a simple survey like this can help a couple begin to understand how each of them is wired and what this could mean in their relationship.

Take, for instance, Brea and Kevin. Brea's survey results revealed a high lion personality type. Kevin, on the other hand, scored high in golden retriever. She was the talkative one; he was the quiet one. She was the natural leader. He was the natural follower.

Could a strong marriage come out of their personality combinations? Yes, but not without mutual effort and understanding. If Brea wanted Kevin to be the leader of their home, she would need to value his gentle and laid-back nature. With her natural potential for dominance and charging ahead, she would need to slow down and work with his "let's talk this out and find a solution that keeps everybody happy" way of doing things. Kevin could benefit from Brea's decisiveness strengths.

Fortunately, in Brea and Kevin's case, Kevin wasn't intimidated by a strong woman but welcomed her gifts and longed to see them reach their full potential. Brea learned to slow down and work with Kevin as they came to decisions *together*. They went on to marry and are successfully learning to allow their different personalities to bring out the best in each other.

PERSPECTIVE DIFFERENCES

I tend to see things in black and white. Bernice, on the other hand, sees life with grays and lots of colors. I've lived long enough to have seen firsthand how much better life is "in living color." My first glimpse of this came when, as a child, I benefited from the color TV Dad bought and brought home for our family to enjoy. Once I began to watch television in color, I never wanted to watch black-and-white TV again.

Marriage has given me a whole new view on life, and I am better for it. Take, for instance, the day I wanted my family to help me with the weekly chores in the yard. I don't particularly like doing yard work, but when it needs to be done, I want to attack the yard and get it done quickly. But I also want it to be done in a specific way. Remember, I'm a lion.

That day is embedded in my memory. I figured with the help of everyone—Bernice, our nine- and six-year-old boys, and our four-year-old daughter—we could get this morning chore knocked out in no time and get on to something far better for the remainder of the day.

My family reluctantly joined me, and we went to work. They proceeded to "help," intermixing their work with a few minutes on the swing set or a couple of trips sliding down the hill in the backyard or picking a flower for Mom. I was not pleased. I wanted them all to focus on the task and do it well, not just "good enough." So I began barking orders and critiquing their work. Then Bernice was not pleased. I could tell by "the look." She was seeing this time of doing yard work together as a family from a different perspective.

Sometime before my yard-work meltdown day, Bernice and I had been discussing the whole matter of perspective and dissonance. Both of us agreed that we wanted to do better at handling life's circumstances and events by thinking of them as fitting somewhere on a scale from one to ten. A ten is something that is really serious and important. A one is something that is an insignificant, minor hiccup in life. If an event was a three, the goal was to recognize it as a three and respond accordingly; that is, not get too upset or emotional about it. If the issue was an eight, it deserved a more serious response.

Well, on that particular yard-work day I blew it. The kids not doing the yard work to my exacting specifications in the scheme of things is probably a two. Maybe less. But I reacted as if it were an eight. The difference between two and eight is dissonance and deserves a big red-letter "WHY?"

The reason I remember that day so vividly is because of Bernice's response. Her more balanced perspective immediately kicked in and helped me learn something about myself that I would have probably missed and that kept me from doing further damage to my children.

Shortly after she gave me the "you are blowing it" look, we had a chance to talk. Actually, she talked. I listened. And I got it. In living color. Yes, the yard work needed to get done, but the interaction we had with our kids that morning was more important than how precisely the lawn was mowed or if every single leaf was picked up. That was a significant growth moment for me. I needed her perspective to help me be the father and husband I long to be.

A GREAT TEAM

As a pastor, over the years I've hired a large number of new staff members for different church positions. At various times, I've been asked to describe the hiring process. My answer is always the same: hiring staff is a lot like dating and marriage.

Great marriages are preceded by a sufficient time of dating that reveals whether you complement each other. Before you hire a new staff member, make sure you've dated long enough to have seen each other's personality strengths and weaknesses. Then when it comes time to make a decision, look for a person who will not only be a great fit but will also add unique value to your team through his or her differences.

If you're thinking about getting engaged, you, too, need to seriously consider your similarities and differences. You need to be an asset, not a deficit to each other. A good relationship isn't only focused on whether or not you can get along with each other. It welcomes the other's differences as assets that will add value to each other's lives. Your relationship should make each of you better individuals because you are better as a couple than you would have been apart.

● BRENT

Earlier in this book, I mentioned that while beginning to get prepared for marriage, I went out and found a mentor. His name is
Roger. He has me get up incredibly early every other week to
meet him for breakfast. So early that if I could see the sun
through the L.A. smog, it would surely just be rising over the
horizon: 8 a.m.

On one of these mornings, I told him about a stretching conversation Danielle and I had had. He said, "Brent, a key step to
knowing when a relationship is legit and going somewhere is
when you start becoming better people from being together. A
big part of this is challenging each other."

Challenging each other? Does that have anything to do with
being better together? With compatibility? Absolutely.

It saddens me to see some of my friends who got married
without really considering the idea that a couple should complement each other through their weaknesses. One of my twenty-
something friends, who is now divorced, shared how this is one
of the big areas he didn't even think about before marriage. They
were a good couple and they loved each other, but the whole
"we challenge each other to be better people and can serve God
better together" thing just didn't even enter into the equation.

I think that's a big mistake. Sure, they claimed they complemented each other, but they didn't address that issue according
to their ministry or work or life goals. They didn't cause each other
to grow at all. They just sought the easy answer and then moved
on toward the wedding. (The easy answer would be, "Yes, of
course we complement each other. We have fun together and
like similar food.")

I don't want to be like that. I don't want to enter an engagement or marriage assuming I'm with someone who complements
me, when in reality that's not the case. I want to make sure I am

with someone who will enhance my ministry for God, and whose ministry I can enhance too. I want to be in a relationship where together we can serve God more effectively than we could alone.

If this chapter asks the question, "Are you better together than apart?" then for me, I think that boils down to three things:

1. *Are we compatible?* Do we get along and have lots of fun together?
2. *Do we complement each other?* Is she good at things I'm hopeless at, and vice versa?
3. *Do we challenge each other?* Are we becoming better people and growing closer to God from being together?

◐ DANIELLE

I love the assurance that God loves me and can use me through being single. I've technically been single all my life (in the sense that I haven't been married before). Still, it's been interesting to see how God can also design a way to show me that I am great when I have someone working alongside me. Brent and I have both grown so much from being with each other, and this is something that often assures me that this relationship is a very good thing.

Ten

● WHAT DOES YOUR HEART SAY?

*E*arlier this year I found the secret for getting seen in a hospital emergency room without sitting forever in the waiting room. I simply used these six words: "I feel pressure in my chest." Those six words got me quickly past every other person who was painfully waiting for medical help.

Not long after I was taken into the treatment area, I learned a second emergency room lesson. Using those six words is also likely to get you a very expensive one-night hospital stay.

Immediately after I was taken into the emergency room treatment area, a doctor came over and asked, "Mr. Gudgel, how do you feel?"

"Well, I feel pretty good," I said, "but my chest has felt strange all day. It could be heartburn. I'm just not sure."

After the doctor had me answer a few more questions, he said, "Your symptoms could be heartburn, but there could also be a problem with your heart. Both have symptoms like the ones you're experiencing. The only way for us to be sure is to run some tests. So with your permission, I am going to send you upstairs and get you started on a series of tests that will determine the cause of the pressure you feel in your chest. Someone will come take you upstairs as soon as a room is available."

"A room? You mean you're going to admit me?"

"Yes. Some of the tests can't be done until tomorrow. So you'll need to stay here overnight. If all is well, you can go home after the tests tomorrow."

"Well, if the tests aren't going to be done until tomorrow, couldn't I just go home and come back tomorrow?"

"Yes, you could do that, but I wouldn't recommend it. We need to know what's causing the pressure you feel. Until we get more information, you're better off staying here where we can monitor you and do the tests. Is that all right with you?"

Frankly, I didn't want to stay overnight at John C. Lincoln Hospital, but I stayed. I'm the kind who would rather be safe than sorry. I've heard or read too many stories about people who died of a heart attack because they ignored similar symptoms. I didn't want to be among their number; at least not yet!

Fortunately for me, after a night in the hospital and what seemed like a thousand tests, I was given good news. My heart was in excellent condition, and they released me. Even though nothing physically had changed, emotionally I felt as if a huge burden had been lifted off my chest.

The state of health your heart is in is not only important for your physical well-being, it's also highly important for your emotional and relational well-being. If you're considering getting engaged, you can't afford to have an irregular relational heartbeat. Rapid maybe, but not irregular. If your heart feels heavy, tense, confused, uneasy, or pressured, you need to find out what's wrong. Something isn't right and it needs to be checked out. It's in your best interest not to ignore any of those relational warning signs.

Look for peace. Not just peace relationally, but peace emotionally too. It's obvious you as a couple need to be at peace with each other. You need to get along. But internal emotional peace is also necessary. It is one of the key ways God reveals His will in our lives.

Paul wrote about the importance of relational and emotional peace in Colossians. He said, "Let the peace of Christ rule in your hearts, since as members of one body you were called to peace."[1]

When Paul used the word *rule*, he had in mind an umpire in the athletic games of his day. To rule was to *act as the umpire* with the final authority. An umpire made the final decision when there was a dispute on the field of play. This person was equivalent to a baseball umpire today. In baseball, the home plate umpire calls the balls and strikes and many of the fair and foul balls. This person, who is also called the umpire-in-chief, is the final authority on the field.

Peace must be the final authority in your heart. Without it you could be making a mistake, thinking you should "play on." Peace is like a relational green flag that tells you to keep on moving forward—full speed ahead. A lack of peace should be like a yellow caution flag. For safety's sake, you need to slow down and proceed with caution. A red flag could be telling you to pull over and stop before you put yourself in harm's way.

WE ALMOST GOT ENGAGED BUT . . .

I could hear the pain in Mark's voice on the other end of the phone when he said, "Not going through with my plan to ask Kim to marry me was the most difficult thing I have ever done."

When I met Mark three years ago, I was immediately impressed. Mark's the kind of guy that you just want to hang around with. Really nice. Considerate. Sharp looking. Smart. Funny. He's a winner, in every sense of the word. Everyone who meets him would love to get to know him better. Kim sure did. After they met, they dated for eighteen months. Their relationship then came to a point where it looked as though Mark was going to ask Kim to marry him. Everyone was expecting it. But instead, he ended up dropping a "we need to break up" bomb.

As Mark and I talked about what happened, I asked, "How close were the two of you to actually getting engaged?"

Mark said, "I was so close to asking Kim to marry me, I had already gone out and bought the engagement ring. I had it in hand. I was that ready to give it to her."

"How old were the two of you at the time?"

"I was thirty, and Kim was twenty-seven."

"Were you in love?"

"Yes, very much so. We had a great relationship."

"Did you communicate well?"

"Yes, we could talk about anything."

"Were you close friends?"

"Yes, possibly even too close. We'd spent all of our time together away from others. We just loved being together and doing things with each other."

"Were you spiritually connected?"

"Yes. God was at the center of our personal lives and also our relationship with each other."

"How was the chemistry between you?" I asked.

"It was great. From the very beginning, we hit it off. When we met on a blind date, we had an immediate connection. We could talk for hours and hours. It seemed like we were the perfect couple."

"Well," I said, "what changed? Why didn't you get engaged?"

"Actually," Mark replied, "it really all boiled down to one thing. I didn't have peace about asking Kim to marry me. Even after I got the engagement ring, I felt like I was making a mistake, like it wasn't the right thing to do. I felt trapped—like I could not in good conscience ask her to marry me. I just didn't have peace about going through with it."

"Wow," I said. "When you began to feel that way, what did you do?"

"Well," Mark replied, "I talked to my dad, and he helped me see the red flags that were waving in front of my face. I also kept praying and asking God for peace. I felt that if He wanted me to marry Kim, He would give me peace before I asked her."

I asked, "Were you ever able to pinpoint a reason for your lack of peace?"

He replied, "Besides the fact that I think it was God who kept me from having peace, which I had been asking Him for, I began to see that when it came to how we saw our lives playing out, Kim and I were different. Kim wanted to settle down and lead a simple, quiet life, raising a family in the Midwest in a nice house with a white picket fence. I wanted something more. I am a risk taker. I like action. I love the big-city West-Coast life. I can't imagine settling down in a small town. I think my lack of peace was directly connected to a mismatch in our core values and what we wanted to do with our lives. So I felt like I needed to accept the fact that we just weren't on the same page. I knew that in my heart. So all of that led to the toughest conversation I've ever had in my life."

When Mark decided not to ask Kim to marry him, I believe he made the right decision, even though it was excruciatingly painful. If Mark had ignored the lack of peace in his heart, he would have made a big mistake. The pain could have multiplied as it did for Bob and Kathy.

WE ALMOST GOT MARRIED BUT . . .

Kathy looked at me with tears in her eyes and pain in her voice and said, "Just six days before our wedding, after being engaged for six months, we called our wedding off. We felt it was the right thing to do, even though it definitely wasn't the easiest thing to do. As you can imagine, it was really hard to make that decision. We had already had two wedding showers, a bachelor party, a bachelorette party, and worse yet, our extended families had already come into town for the wedding. Some of them had flown in that week from other states. But in spite of all that, we knew if we went through with the ceremony, we would have been making a huge mistake. So we called it off."

Three years earlier, Bob and Kathy had met at a popular local restaurant. They, along with sixty other twenty-somethings, had come there to eat dinner and hear about a singles' study their church was starting, related to dating and marriage. As single adults who were *looking*, this study sounded as if it could be helpful and a lot of fun.

As it turned out, they ended up not needing that study to find their special one. After that night, it seemed that they might be a perfect match for each other. In the two weeks that followed, they went out on a couple of dates. After those two dates, they decided they weren't ready for a serious relationship with each other, so they made a commitment to "just be friends."

Over the next year, Bob and Kathy's friendship grew. Since they enjoyed each other's company, it was only natural for them to continue their friendship by e-mail and phone when Bob went away to college. It is said that absence makes the heart grow fonder, and that certainly was the case with Bob and Kathy. Although they were living in separate cities, the distance actually drew them closer together. Their e-mails and phone calls changed their relationship from being that of just friends to being each other's boyfriend and girlfriend.

After a year away at school, Bob moved back home and continued dating Kathy, in person. This time they hit it off and seriously dated each other for the next year and a half. Their dating ultimately led to engagement, which was followed by six months of preparation for their wedding.

Everyone who knew them thought they were perfect for each other. That, in part, was what made it so hard for them when they began to feel that they shouldn't get married.

"When did you begin to have doubts about whether or not you should get married?" I asked Kathy.

"Three weeks after we got engaged," Kathy said.

"What happened?" I asked.

Kathy replied, "We were on a three-week trip together. It was actually a trip where we were ministering together in a third-world country. A few days into the trip, I began to see a side of Bob that I had not seen before. We started having conflicts. Huge conflicts. We were far from meshing in our ministry together. I also began to realize that if I married Bob, because of these conflicts, I wouldn't be able to do what I believe God made me to do. So I began to feel like red flags were popping up all over the place."

"So what did you do after that trip to deal with your feelings?" I asked.

"We talked about it when we got back to the States, and we also brought it up in our premarital counseling sessions because both of us were feeling like we shouldn't get married."

"What did your counselors say?"

"The couple who was doing our counseling said that what we were feeling was probably from Satan—that he would try to rip us apart by attacking our feelings. And then the wife added, 'I've heard from the Lord. You're supposed to be married.'"

When I heard Kathy tell me that, my heart sank. This may be strong, but as a pastor who does a lot of premarital counseling, I'd call that stupid advice. After I shared with Kathy my feelings about the counsel they received, I said, "So how did you respond to their advice?"

She replied, "Their counsel pretty much calmed us down for a while. But then some other issues came up. I once again began to seriously question if I should marry Bob. I began to see more things in him and in our relationship that gave me uneasy feelings about going forward. After a couple more months, it finally came to a point where we both agreed to take a day off from our jobs and just pray about whether or not we should go through with the wedding. At the end of that day, both of us knew we couldn't get married. Neither one of us had peace that this was the right thing to do. So we called it off."

"Kathy," I said, "I think you did the right thing—even though it was the hard thing to do. In spite of what your counselors said, whom I disagree with, you did the right thing. I believe God uses peace, or the lack of it, as a way of showing us His will."

After Kathy and I spent some time talking about how she is doing now, I asked, "If you were to help someone who is struggling with 'should I or shouldn't I go through with getting engaged or married?' what would you say to them now?"

Without hesitation she replied, "I'd tell them to pay attention to what your heart says. If you don't have peace, don't get engaged until you do. And if you're already engaged, don't make a mistake and get married, no matter how hard it might be to call it off."

I agree with Kathy 100 percent.

● BRENT

I can relate to these "lack of peace" stories on way too many levels.

The first year of Danielle's and my relationship, we seemed to be on a fast track to getting married. We both just felt that was the direction we were headed. We were so excited that our conversations often got the best of us, and before we knew it, we were talking dates for engagement and a wedding.

Frankly, it was a lot of fun to talk about. We enjoyed thinking about getting married and saying things in unison like, "Oh, all the happy times we will have together."

The day I realized I was lacking peace was the day we visited a jeweler to size engagement rings. When that sample ring was slipped over Danielle's finger, she could not hold back her excitement. She had one of those rare smiles where there is so much joy inside that it is impossible to hide or stop it.

I have only seen this kind of smile in two other places: 1) at a friend's wedding on the bride's face when vows were being said—she couldn't hold back the happiness, and 2) on my face when I shot a handgun for the first time—it was as if I was a kid again. Weird.

As we looked at the rings, my heart sank in confusion. I was so happy with her, but I wasn't *that* happy. I wanted to be *that* happy. To have that uncontrollable smile. I told myself things like: *I must be adjusting to being in a real, serious relationship. That's all this is; it's me moving past an old way toward a future of commitment. I'll get over it.*

And, *We're just going through a rough spot. It will pass.* And *This isn't a lack of peace; it's just a natural process . . .*

You see, it is so fun and easy to get carried away in the excitement of getting married. So easy to make plans. It's much harder to be honest when what's going on is so confusing. Honesty has the potential to disrupt the flow of a beautiful impending engagement. I worried that if I said something, I would ruin everything, so I reasoned that maybe I just shouldn't say anything.

Questions like these flooded my mind as worry crept in. I began to pray a lot about this, and just like the water turned into wine, a miracle happened for our relationship. God resolved everything.

Danielle broke up with me.

OK, she kind of broke up with me. Danielle courageously shared how she had this thing nagging her on a deep level (see also: lack of peace) that she couldn't figure out. But she *had* to figure it out.

This news lifted a huge burden off my chest. Danielle shared what I was too scared to, and it turned out we both felt the lack of peace. When she tried that ring on, her huge smile was because this was the fulfillment of a childhood dream, not because she was totally at peace. I kidded about my smiling holding a gun earlier, but it's kind of similar. Boys play army and pretend they have guns when they're young; girls perform dating and marriage rituals with their dolls.

Danielle and I left that conversation in agreement; we felt a lack of peace and needed to figure it out. But we didn't feel a peace about ending things either. We decided not to break up but not to be together either. We would be in relational purgatory with no definition on how to get out.

The time to pretend we felt at peace was over.

WE DID GET MARRIED BUT . . .

It's been twenty-eight years now since my brother Greg got married. Unfortunately, it's also been almost twenty-seven years since Greg got divorced. Their marriage only lasted several months. To this day, when you talk to Greg about what happened, he will tell you he should have listened to his heart. Had he paid attention to what his heart was saying, he would have never gotten married.

Greg can still remember the conversation he and I had in the final minutes before his wedding ceremony. We were sitting in the choir room in the back of the church waiting for the ceremony to begin. Just before we were to walk out, Greg turned to me and said, "Dave, I'm making a mistake by marrying Becky."

Somewhat surprised, I said, "What do you mean?"

Greg replied, "I just don't have peace about this. I'm just not sure I'm doing the right thing."

At that time I was young enough and naïve enough to say, "No, Greg, you're just nervous. Everything will be fine." I'd never say that now, especially if I had at the time known the rest of the story.

Greg's story started heading for trouble several weeks before his wedding day, when he began to feel as though he shouldn't get married. The unsettled feeling in his heart got so strong that he finally set up a special appointment to meet with the pastor who had done their premarital counseling.

After Greg sat down in the pastor's office, he said, "I don't think I should go through with the wedding."

When Greg told me this part of the story, he said, "After I said that, the pastor looked at me and said, 'Greg, don't you believe God brought the two of you together?'"

"So what did you say to him?" I inquired.

Greg said, "I told him yes, and then he said, 'Well then, why can't you believe now that in the same way God brought the two of you together, if He doesn't want you married, He will break you up?'"

Greg told me it made him feel as though he lacked faith. So he just listened and accepted what the pastor said. And went through with the wedding.

They say hindsight is 20/20. If you ask me, I think God was trying to say to Greg, "Call it off. Don't go through with this. You're not ready to be married. Hit the brakes before it's too late."

The message of this chapter is simple: If your heart is experiencing turmoil and uncertainty, call time-out. Stop and find out why it's feeling that way. It may be a sign from God to spare you from a potential coming disaster.

On the other hand, if your heart is at peace and rest, that's good. That's a sign that you may be ready to move forward with the relationship. Press on. Something good may be in the future for you as a couple.

Remember Mark? The one who almost got engaged but didn't? He's engaged now and will be married soon. Not to Kim, whom he broke up with, but to Christine. I talked to him about this new relationship recently and asked, "Do you have peace this time?"

Mark replied, "This time I have complete peace about marrying Christine. When I went out and bought the ring, my heart was filled with excitement, joy, and peace. The contrast between how I feel now and how I felt with Kim is night and day. This time I know I'm doing the right thing."

That's exactly how you need to feel. Fully at peace. Pay attention to your heart. It could be the difference between relational life and death.

● BRENT

So Danielle and I didn't break up, but we weren't together. It was that whole cliché—sometimes you have to let your love go. If they come back, then they really do love you.

We had to give our relationship up to God completely. Even if it meant we might not end up together. We wanted to be together, and we felt we could ultimately end up together, but there was this unrest, and we just had to figure it out. And that meant giving each other space. It meant venturing into the unknown, relationally. It was scary, but we both knew it was absolutely the right thing.

To rush things would have been so wrong for our relationship. Rushing things almost ended it, and if we had continued on that path, I'm scared to think what would have happened after we got married.

We had been lying to ourselves, thinking we felt peace. We lied to ourselves, thinking we were pursuing something so beautiful, so perfect. Something we felt we were destined to do. Something we felt we were told by God would happen.

After a few weeks, we gradually started to heal. After a few months, the unrest began to disappear. Now things in our relationship are completely different, and we're not making the mistake of planning a wedding before it's even time to get engaged. Just because we felt early on in our relationship that we would end up together didn't mean it was right to rush things. I now realize we initially took things into our own hands under our own timing. We claimed we were waiting on God's timing, but really it was our selfish timing. Our relationship wasn't wrong, but our plans were.

Maybe this doesn't make sense as you read it. Maybe you feel at total peace in your relationship, and if that's so, then that's awesome. Enjoy it! I really mean it.

But if you feel like Danielle and I did, my advice would be this: really seek God first. Don't make any rash decisions. Just pray and be open to what He has in store. And then wait.

Now Danielle and I are on a rather enjoyable path of patient rebuilding. We're taking it slowly, and we are completely at peace with that.

◉ DANIELLE

Oh, this is a good chapter. My heart has said a lot of things in my relationship with Brent, but one thing it said the most through that first year was "wait." I had gotten ahead of myself and desperately needed to listen to that message. I always felt that message was from God, but I just wasn't listening. Probably because that's not what I wanted to hear. Now, many months later, things are very different. I have learned to listen to my heart better, which in turn makes the whole process of growing in a relationship and ultimately considering engagement much more fun.

Part 3

WHAT DO
OTHERS THINK?

Eleven

◉ CONSIDER WHAT GOD SAYS

I'm a sucker for infomercials. That's why a UPS man showed up one day at our doorstep with a package that contained "the perfect car washing soap," which I had purchased after watching my *last* infomercial. I say *last* because it was not only the last in a row of infomercials I had seen, it was also the last infomercial Bernice allowed me to see before she said, "That's it."

When she answered the doorbell, saw a UPS man heading back out to his truck, and found a large brown mystery package sitting on the porch, she asked, "Dave . . . what is this?"

"It's . . . a secret," I replied.

"Oh, really. [Insert "the look" here.] What's in the box?"

I knew I'd been had. "Well, I was watching this infomercial

about the world's best car washing soap, and the experts say this stuff is really good. It's guaranteed not to streak, it doesn't harm the environment, it even gets off grease and sap. And it leaves the car looking brand-new. Doesn't that sound great? And they offered this incredible deal if we called in within the next thirty minutes. So, I decided it would be a good thing to do." (By the way, it's been ten years since I made that purchase, and we still have almost all of the soap left. It's stored out in the garage . . . with a number of other infomercial purchases from pre-banning days.)

With "the look" still on her face, she said, "You know what, Dave? You are *infomercial challenged.* I think we need to add a second item to your 'Things Dave Is Not Allowed to Do Anymore' list." (This list was started when I was banned from playing soccer and baseball after the local emergency room personnel began to say, "Hi, Dave" as I walked in the door.) "From here on out, no more infomercials."

I've done pretty well with my infomercial ban, but I still have free reign to look at ads. That's why when I was recently doing some research for this book, I ran across an ad online for "expert dating advice." When I saw the following header, I had to know more:

Wish you knew someone who knows everything about dating?

It sounded as if someone was claiming to know everything about dating. Everything? *Right.* The ad went on to say:

Now you do. 30,000 skilled professionals are ready to give you immediate advice or assistance on any conceivable topic, live via chat or email. It's fast, affordable, and you'll wonder how you've ever managed without it.[1]

That was enough to pique my curiosity and send me on a little exploratory journey to find out what a "skilled dating professional" looks like. So I clicked in and was taken to a page that had thirty headshots. Each person had a brief bio and, as a dating expert, was ready to help me with whatever dating questions or problems I might have. All I had to do was decide which one or more of these experts I wanted to ask for advice.

Would I choose Anne Marie McNell at a cost of fifty cents a minute, or Psychic Readings by Sophia at twenty dollars a minute? If these two didn't seem right for me, I could go with one of the twenty-eight others whose prices fell between these two dating experts. (Interesting that the most expensive one was a psychic. Not really relevant, but interesting.)

So-called expert advice is readily available on the Web. Recently I discovered that when I Googled the words "expert advice," I was given 42,800,000 places I could go for expert advice on just about anything.

With my *sucker* buying tendencies, I'm probably not the best person for determining who among the forty-two million would truly qualify as experts. But I do think I can accurately say, of all the experts you could consult, God is on the top of the expert list—especially when it comes to relationships. And I believe that applies to an engagement decision. Before you decide to get engaged, seek His advice first.

I REALLY WANT TO KNOW WHAT GOD THINKS

"OK," you say, "but how do I go about getting His advice? After all, I can't sit down and talk with Him and have a two-way conversation. And I'm pretty sure I'm not going to find a verse in the Bible that says, 'Jeremy should marry Lindsey.'" So how does a person go about consulting with God about whom they should marry?

It would be nice if it were as simple as going to a Web site and typing in a question, knowing that God would reply with the perfect answer. Since no one can do that, people often turn to pastors like me for help in sorting out God's will for a variety of situations. This happens a lot when someone is trying to get a grasp on His will regarding getting engaged and married.

Perhaps you can relate to this son who wrote his dad and said:

> Dad,
>
> I am writing to ask you to please pray for me and ask some key people that you know to do the same. Lindsey and I are both of the mind that we want God's direction in our life and that we want more than anything else to be walking in His will. To that end, over the weekend we are going to have a communication fast to spend time in prayer and seek God's leading.
>
> I will admit I am torn as to how I should pray. A huge part of me wants to spend hours and hours on my knees praying that our relationship will move forward and that God will help that. However, I know that I should pray that God would reveal His will to both of us and that we would have the faith and confidence to follow that leading, no matter where it takes us. I would ask that you pray for me, for Lindsey, and that God would make His direction clear to both of us and then allow us to move forward with purpose and determination.
>
> Thank you. Talk to you soon.
>
> Love,
>
> Jeremy

I think Jeremy's letter is great. It's honest, open, and right on track. He sincerely wants to know and do God's will. So he turned to prayer and asked for his father to join him in praying that God would make His will clear. He also asked that his dad ask a few other key people to join him in this prayer. That's why his father wrote me and said:

> Pastor Dave,
>
> I would like you and Bernice to be two of the "key people" who pray for Jeremy and Lindsey this week and weekend. I am encouraged by how they are approaching this, and Nancy and I are praying diligently for God's will and for His wisdom for them.
>
> If God leads you to send Jeremy some word of wisdom and encouragement, that would be great, as will your prayers. They are trying to avoid an endless "dating" situation and are giving serious consideration to the next step, which would be engagement. They just want to be sure.
>
> Thank you!
> Frank

If I had been that dad, I would have done the same thing. God knows best, so the best thing we can do is ask Him to show us what is best.

GOD IS READY TO REVEAL HIS WILL

I have often joined others in praying that God's will and wisdom will be known, because I believe "the LORD gives wisdom, and from his mouth come knowledge and understanding."[2] When we don't know, He does. God has promised to give whatever wisdom is needed when we, by faith, pray and ask for His help. James made this clear when he said, "If any of you lacks wisdom, he should ask God, who gives generously to all without finding fault, and it will be given to him."[3]

There will never be a day when God says to you or anyone

else who asks for His expert advice: "You again? Haven't you figured this out yet? Go away. Don't bother Me. I have more important things to do than help you sort out your engagement decision. It's just not that important to Me."

No, God will never say something like that! If something is important to you, it's important to Him. He is ready to help.

Sometimes we think of God's will as a carrot being dangled in front of a donkey, always just out of reach. As if He's saying, "Ha! Just try to figure out what I want you to do." But that's not how God works. He wants you to know His will. He longs to give you . . .

- *knowledge*—what the right or best thing to do is;
- *wisdom*—how and when something should be done;
- *understanding*—what this all means in your particular circumstances.

So ask Him.

It was an honor for me to join Jeremy and Frank in praying that God would make His will clear. I jotted a short note back to Frank and told him he could count on my prayers. Frank in turn passed my response along to Jeremy, but before I wrote back with any "words of wisdom," Jeremy contacted me directly. He wrote:

Pastor Dave,

I really appreciate your willingness to pray for Lindsey and me as we go through this time. I am comforted by the knowledge that my extended Christian family is involved and praying. I was wondering if you had any thoughts or key scriptures about discerning God's will and seeking His leading, most especially in a romantic relationship. Lindsey and

I have experienced some great adventures, have made strong emotional and spiritual connections, and are developing powerful feelings for each other. We are committed to following God's leadership and seeking His direction before we move much further in our commitment to each other.

> Thank you for all of your support.
>
> Jeremy

I love getting this kind of letter. Not because I have all the answers; I don't. But I have done some serious thinking about this area and have often suggested that along with prayer, knowing God's *unrevealed will* is connected to doing His *revealed will*. In this case, after I said a little prayer, I wrote Jeremy back and said this:

Hi, Jeremy,

I am excited for both of you as God continues to lead in your lives. Sorting out a relationship that could go on to engagement and marriage is never just plainly obvious. But I find comfort in Psalm 37:4. If your will is lined up with God's will, then your desires will be His desires. In other words, God's unrevealed will about the future of your relationship with Lindsey will be made clear as you are willing to obey His revealed will.

I am excited to see what's next in your lives.

> God bless,
>
> Dave Gudgel

YOU CAN KNOW GOD'S UNREVEALED WILL

Before you nail me for offering too simple an answer, let me explain. The essence of what I believe is this—I think the best way to know God's *unrevealed will* (Should Jeremy and Lindsey get married?) is understood in doing God's *revealed will*. If you seek to do God's *revealed will*, your desires will be in line with His desires. At that point, you can act on your desires with full assurance that they are in line with God's will.

If what I just said made you say, "Huh?" I understand. Stay with me for a moment, and I will try to make this important truth clear.

Psalm 37:4 is one of my favorite verses in the Bible. It says, "Delight yourself in the LORD and he will give you the desires of your heart." I believe this verse contains three key elements in knowing God's will:

1. *You must first delight yourself in the Lord.* This simply means taking pleasure in God and His revealed will for your life. Make pleasing God, obeying Him in the areas where He has spoken clearly, and living for Him your life's pursuit. It was obvious that this was Jeremy's desire when he wrote, "We are committed to following God's leadership and seeking His direction."

2. If you delight yourself in the Lord, *God will put His desires in your heart.* Your thinking will be in line with His thinking. What He wants will be what you want. Your will will be in line with His will. When this is the case . . .

3. *You can act in accord with the desires God has placed in your heart.* This is possible because when you live out God's revealed will, your desires will be in line with His unrevealed will.

Let me make this as simple as I can. If you're contemplating engagement, make the same commitment Jeremy did. Make sure that you are walking in obedience to God in the areas where He clearly gives us direction in the Bible. Then ask Him to make your desires line up with His in the relationship with the person you are considering marrying. Then follow your heart.

If this is your desire, you need to pay special attention to three areas where God's revealed will is absolutely clear. I believe prayer, along with obedience in these areas, will help you sort out God's unrevealed will in your engagement decision. The three areas to focus on are: salvation, spirit-filling, and sanctification.

Are You Saved for Sure?

First, before you can know God's will, you need to be *saved*. Salvation makes a personal relationship with God possible. Without the forgiveness that is found in God's Son, Jesus Christ, our sin separates us from God.

The first and most important step in knowing God's will is a step of faith in Jesus Christ. When anyone willingly turns from sin to Christ for salvation, the sin separation between God and man is removed. From this point on, one is in a position to know and experience God's will.

Once you have taken this step, you will be connected to God and will begin enjoying the fruit of a personal relationship with Him. I hope if you haven't taken this step, you will now. The Bible clearly reveals this is God's first will for your life when it says He is "not willing that any should perish but that all should come to repentance."[4]

Are You Filled with God's Spirit?

After salvation, we know it's God's will for His children to live *spirit-filled* lives. The apostle Paul said, "Therefore do not be foolish, but understand what the Lord's will is. Do not get drunk on wine, which leads to debauchery. Instead, be filled with the Spirit."[5]

Instead of living under the influence of alcohol, it's God's desire that His followers live under the influence of the Holy Spirit. The degree to which you experience God's influence or complete control in your life is directly connected to biblical transformation, total surrender, and ongoing confession of sin.

When our minds are *transformed* by God's Word, our thoughts will be in line with God's will. When our wills are completely *surrendered* to obeying God, our actions will be completely in line with God's will.

When we sin against God and grieve the Holy Spirit by doing things that are contrary to God's will, or quench the Holy Spirit by ignoring His leadings and promptings, our hearts are not in line with God's heart. But when we acknowledge our sin and confess it as wrong, our hearts *will* be in line with His. Seeking to walk in the Spirit, moment by moment and day by day, which at times means *confessing sin* and asking for forgiveness, is absolutely essential to knowing God's will.

Are You Practicing Sanctification?

Sanctification is the third key to knowing God's will. The Bible says, "It is God's will that you should be sanctified: that you should avoid sexual immorality; that each of you should learn to control his own body in a way that is holy and honorable."[6]

As I've already suggested earlier in this book, maintaining sexual purity may be the greatest challenge you or any other dating couple will face. This is especially true in our culture, where polls show that the majority of people believe sex before marriage is normal.

If you're serious about wanting to know God's unrevealed will, you need to decide to obey His revealed will regarding sexual purity. His desire is that you be sanctified, which in this area means to be completely set apart from sexual immorality. Controlling your sexual passions will not only please God, it will assure you of God's will.

If you give in to your physical desires in this area where God has made His *revealed will* clear, not only will your desires be outside of God's desires, but you will also put yourself in a place of greater uncertainty about God's *unrevealed will*. The physical can do more to deceive you into thinking you should get married than any other area in your relationship.

GOD'S REVEALED WILL IS THE PATHWAY TO HIS UNREVEALED WILL

Taking all that I've suggested in this chapter and applying it in Jeremy's situation, here's how all this relates. The best way for Jeremy to know if he should marry Lindsey (God's unrevealed will) is by praying that God will make His will clear as he is obedient to God's revealed will.

Since Jeremy and Lindsey were already saved in the past and are now experiencing a relationship with God, their focus should be on two key areas. First, *walking in the spirit*, which at its core means living for God's will. It's the attitude of heart that Jeremy reflected in his letters. A "Your will, not mine" mentality.

This desire can be expressed in words like, "Lord, show me what You want. All I want is what You want. When I blow it, please show me my sin so I can make it right with You and get back on track. I want to live for Your will, not mine. I want my desires to be in line with Yours."

Jeremy and Lindsey also need to keep *walking in purity*. As they maintain moral and sexual purity in their relationship, their desires will line up with God's. If they are like most couples, this may be the most difficult area to keep under control, but as they do, they will enjoy God's best and be assured of God's plan for their lives.

So once again, knowing God's unrevealed will—should Jeremy marry Lindsey?—is best accomplished through prayer and obeying God's revealed will. If you delight yourself in God's revealed will, your desires will be in line with His desires. His unrevealed will will be made clear through your desires (which should be considered in light of the other principles already looked at in this book).

If you can say that you are committed to asking God to make His unrevealed will known to you, and to obeying God's revealed will, then my question for you is simple: "What are your desires telling you about what you should do?" Are they giving you a green, yellow, or red light?

❯ BRENT

After I graduated from college, I was hired to go on a photo tour throughout Southeast Asia for a client. It was basically a senior trip where I got paid to take pictures in Vietnam, Laos, Cambodia, Thailand, China, and Tibet. A pretty incredible opportunity.

The journey started out with my flying alone to Vietnam. Upon arrival I got my passport stamped and exited the airport through one of those gauntlets with all the locals waiting for arriving passengers. I scanned the crowd for my local contacts, who would be holding a sign with my name on it and would be taking care of me. After five minutes of frantically searching, though, I came to a startling realization: nobody was there to pick me up.

I found a place to sit and began to pray. *God, where are they? Please help me.*

I tried calling, but the emergency numbers I was given were

wrong numbers. I sat and prayed more. *God, help me. Please show me what to do. Give me an answer.*

Hours passed. More prayer.

Why wasn't God helping me? Why wouldn't He reveal a way out? I was waiting and waiting for Him to show me, but He wasn't. I couldn't figure it out. Six hours after being stranded, it finally hit me. Maybe I should just do something.

I went over to an airport help counter that I had been to several times earlier without finding any help, because nobody spoke English. Except this time I was greeted by a new lady who inexplicably spoke English. And her name was Thang Kyu. Yes, her name was pronounced "thank you." Holding down my excitement, I began to share my situation: "Hi, I got left here and I need to get into the city and to a hotel, but don't even know how to get a taxi driver to take me to Hanoi."

"Oh, OK. No problem," she replied while pulling out a AAA guidebook. "Where would you like to stay?" Relief swept over me as I picked a nice hotel, which Thang Kyu then booked for me and guided me into a taxi to get me there.

I had sat at the airport for six hours waiting for someone to guide me. Waiting for God to tell me what to do. Begging Him. But maybe all He wanted me to do was to take a step. If I hadn't taken a step, I might still be sitting in that airport, waiting for God to lay the path out in front of me, grab my hand, and then walk me through it.

I think it is absolutely necessary to consult God. I love the concept that by walking in the Spirit we can discern God's undisclosed will, sometimes simply by making a choice. It can be dangerous to make a decision too hastily or without consulting God. It can also be dangerous when we wait and wait and wait for God to hit us over the head with an answer. Sometimes I think we know what we need to do and just have to take the next step.

IF YOU'RE LOOKING FOR A SOUL MATE

Often the matter of a soul mate is thrown into a discussion about God's will for whom you should marry. A soul mate is thought to be the one perfect person for you—someone God created specifically for you to find and marry. And if you don't find that person, you will never experience the perfect relationship God had planned for you.

In a study done by the National Marriage Project at Rutgers University, it was found that 94 percent of never-married single adults, ages twenty to twenty-nine years old, say, "When you marry, you want your spouse to be your soul mate, first and foremost."[7] That belief has produced a lot of anxiety for some people who feel pressure to find that one perfect person whom God made just for them.

If this concept of "one perfect soul mate" is true, with 6.6 billion people in the world, the chance of not finding that special one is huge! How many people have you dated? Four? Ten? *Hmm.* That means you have a couple billion more guys or girls to check out before you find your one perfect Prince Charming or Sleeping Beauty. And what if you make a mistake?

The "I found the one perfect person for me" myth can create problems in a marriage. When marital conflict comes along—and it will—that myth can cause you to question if you truly did find the one. "Maybe I missed the perfect match God made in heaven for me. Maybe I made a mistake. Why didn't I keep looking? Now I'm stuck with what feels like second or third best."

Here's what you need to know about finding a soul mate: nowhere in the pages of Scripture can you find even a suggestion that God made one special person for you to marry. But even if He did, how would you know who that one is? The same way we've been talking about in this chapter.

In some ways, the soul mate issue is a moot point. Soul mate or not, you only want to marry someone who will become your soul mate. And the best way to know that for sure is found in getting God's expert advice, which He will reveal to you as you pray and walk in His revealed will.

TO BRIAN FROM YOUR DAD

When my son Brian and his then-girlfriend, now wife, Mary, began considering marriage, I wanted to help them be sure they had an accurate reading on God's will for their lives. So I wrote a dad-to-son letter. Here's a part of that letter:

Hi, Brian,

Over the past couple of months I have often thought about you and your relationship with Mary. Of course as your dad I want what is best for you, and therefore have spent a lot of time praying for you and whatever the future holds. I'm guessing that you will probably choose to get married someday, and if Mary is the one, my prayer is that you will experience God's best, both before and after marriage.

My hope in writing is to encourage you to hang on to God's best counsel and not give in to sexual intimacy before marriage. As your dad, and I hope as your friend—and if you'd like, as a pastor who has worked with hundreds of couples—I long to see you experience God's best. If I could point to my own experience, I'd say I am so glad that your mom and I did not give in to premarital sex. I really believe the great marriage we have now, and have had all these years, is directly connected to the relationship we had before we married and our strong desire to obey His Word.

At the risk of giving you a lecture, which is something I

don't want to do (and hopefully something that I have rarely ever done with you), I hope you won't mind me giving you the two best pieces of counsel I give to couples who are in serious relationships that could lead to marriage.

First, your goal should be to know God's unrevealed will. But the key to knowing His unrevealed will is to obey His revealed will. For me the big question when I was dating your mom was, Is it God's will for me to marry Bernice? I call that His unrevealed will because I can't look anywhere in the Bible and find "Dave, it's My will that you marry Bernice." But I could find many clear revealed will statements like 1 Thessalonians 4:3 that says, "For this is the *will* of God, your sanctification; that is, that you abstain from sexual immorality" [NASB].

In other words, for me to be sure of God's unrevealed will, I needed to hold myself back sexually, because I *knew* that was His will. By obeying God in this area, along with other areas where He makes His will clear, I would be in a place to know God's will concerning marriage, because my desires would line up with God's desires (Psalm 37:4). By living a life of disobedience, I would put myself in a place where I wouldn't have a clue what God's will was for me in marriage. This is especially true related to sex, since it can easily deceive people into thinking they should get married.

Second, as you date, focus on building spiritual, emotional, and relational intimacy. Again, hold off on physical intimacy until after you marry. I really think this is a key to marrying the right person and experiencing a great marriage. Unfortunately, most couples get this messed up, and it results in marriage being so little of what it could be and so often ending in divorce.

I believe one of the reasons God set this design in place

was to protect couples from deep residual pain and to give them the best marriages possible. Couples who are considering marriage should focus on building:

> spiritual intimacy with each other and God,
> emotional intimacy, by growing in their understanding of each other, and
> relational intimacy, by developing a deep friendship.

Together, these factors will not only help them know if they should get married, but will also give them a solid foundation on which they can build a strong marriage. Without these three things, their relationship will be shallow at best, and will hang by a thin thread of sexual intimacy for happiness. While sexual intimacy is important in a marriage, it alone will never be able to sustain a relationship through the challenges that all couples will face.

Brian, I love you and long for you to experience God's best. I know your walk with God is important to you. I am so thankful for that. But I also know that Satan is a roaring lion and would love to devour you by stealing life away from you rather than allowing you to experience all the life that God offers.

I will keep praying for your strength and your ability to resist temptation. If you can do that, through God's power and strength, and your application of His Word, I know you will put yourself in a place to experience God's blessing. And one day, if you decide to marry, your desires will line up with God's desires, and you will get your married life off to the greatest start possible. I can hardly wait to see all that this could mean in your life.

I love you. Keep walking worthy.

Dad

My hope for you is the same one I had for Brian: that you would clearly know God's unrevealed will. I believe that will be made clear to you as you seek to obey His revealed will.

● BRENT

Since the beginning of my relationship with Danielle, I have been praying this prayer: *Lord, be the center of our relationship.*

It makes sense to pray about "us." I want God to be the center. I want to make sure we're seeking His will. But in actuality, is having God at the center of a relationship easier said than done?

Lord, please be the center of our relationship. May Your will be done, not ours. Help us follow You.

This seems like a good prayer, but in my life I've found that it's sometimes too easy to pray that prayer. I've found that sometimes it doesn't really mean much. So many times I was praying this and wanting to seek God, but in reality I was still putting my own selfish decisions before God's. I have found it's easy to tell God you want Him to be first or to be the center, but it's an entirely different thing to actually want that.

How about this prayer instead: *Lord, may this relationship be about You and Your desires, not mine or ours. If our desires are getting in the way of Your plan, I ask that You change us. If our relationship is not of You, I ask that You end it. If it is of You, I ask that You bless it and use it. We give it to You. Help us to seek You always and to figure out what that means in this relationship.*

It was a prayer like this that changed everything for Danielle and me. It's a harder prayer. Through this time when we're seriously dating and trying to figure out if we should ultimately get engaged, it has become abundantly clear that the harder prayer is the better prayer for our relationship.

The harder prayers are scary. They acknowledge that His will really is better. They acknowledge submission, even if it means giving up everything that you currently love. This is His ideal for us. This is the better way.

Before, I prayed the simple prayer, and it allowed me to feel as though I was submitting our relationship to God when I wasn't really. Now I know I need to continually seek His better way. Even when everything is going great with Danielle and me, even when we are so in love, I still must acknowledge it's His plan and not mine that I'm seeking.

Twelve

● CONSIDER WHAT YOUR FRIENDS AND FAMILY SAY

I'm a golfer. At least that's what I like to think. Over the thirty years I've played golf, I've had my share of good and bad rounds. To be accurate, even though I am a pretty good golfer, the number of times I've played bad golf has far outweighed the number of times I've played good golf. That makes me your typical amateur golfer—frustrated more often than elated about his game. Not long ago my frustration finally drove me to ask Tyler, at Kirkendoll Golf Institute, for some help.

Prior to contacting Tyler, I had watched him help many professional and amateur golfers. Even from a distance I could see he knew what he was doing. He was highly capable of pin-pointing swing problems and prescribing suitable solutions.

That's why, when my wife asked me last year what I wanted for Christmas, I said, "I'd just like one thing. Golf lessons with Tyler. I need professional help." Santa was good to me, and shortly after Christmas, Tyler and I got together.

My first golf lesson with Tyler took place in his golf studio. Before he took me outside, he wanted to work with me inside, where both of us could observe my golf swing. Tyler's studio is fully equipped with two different video cameras that record a golf swing from two different angles. And since the camera doesn't lie, it's an important tool in Tyler's swing-repair arsenal. When he uses it to replay someone's golf swing, it's pretty easy to see flaws. Mine had a lot. After only two swings, Tyler stopped me from hitting more balls and said, "Come over here. I want to replay your swing for you and show you what you'll need to do if you want to improve." What came next was a shock.

I had no idea how bad my golf swing was. Let's just say I could keep Tyler in business for a long time! But the thing that got me the most was that I had thought my golf swing was pretty good. Without Tyler's expert observations and the actual swing replays, I never would have seen what was wrong.

What I was actually doing in my swing was not even close to what I thought I was doing. But now the truth stared me in the face. Much improvement was needed. If I was going to make further progress, I needed to learn from what Tyler saw and the cameras revealed. To ignore that would be just plain foolish if I hoped to make significant improvements in my golf game.

WE ALL HAVE BLIND SPOTS

So what does my golf swing have to do with preengagement? Primarily this: everyone has blind spots. There are areas in my life and in your life that are blind to us but often not to others. Sometimes these issues are small and, for the most part, insignificant—like trying to improve a golf swing. Other times the blind spots are huge and potentially detrimental, especially when they connect with a lifelong decision like marriage. What's amazing is that these areas of blindness can continue to go unseen by us until we have the input of others. I guess that's why they call them blind spots.

In 1955 Joseph Luft and Harry Ingham created a metaphorical tool called a Johari window, to help people understand how we perceive ourselves and others.[1] Their four-paned window, as illustrated below, divides perception into four quadrants: open, hidden, blind, and unknown.

OPEN	BLIND
I see Others see	I don't see Others see
HIDDEN	UNKNOWN
I see Others don't see	I don't see Others don't see

The *open* quadrant represents areas that you and others know about you. The *hidden* pane contains the things in your life that you know about, but others don't. The areas in your life that are a mystery to you and others are in the *unknown* box. The *blind* quadrant represents what others clearly see, but you don't see.

My concern here is with the blind part of our lives. The list of potential blind spots is endless:

- You may think of yourself as open to input, but others see you as closed.
- You may think of yourself as a good listener, but others see you as inattentive.
- You may think of yourself as loving, but others see you as uncaring and removed.
- You may think of yourself as responsible, but others see you as irresponsible.

WE NEED EACH OTHER'S INPUT

As I mentioned earlier, soon after God created man, He made woman because, as Genesis says, "It is not good for the man to be alone. I will make a helper suitable for him."[2] When that statement was made, Adam was perfect and he was living in a perfect world. Yet even then, God said man needed companionship. He needed help in order to realize his full potential.

We can be sure if the first man needed help *before* sin entered the world, men all the more need help now *after* sin has entered the world. We need supportive people in our lives who can encourage us and help us push past our sinful imperfections. Much of this help is derived through the counsel we can give and receive from one another.

Wise people, in contrast to fools, seek out others' input and counsel. They know they don't have all the answers or have everything all together. They know they have blind spots and need the valuable input that others can give. They agree with the Proverbs that say, "As iron sharpens iron, so one man sharpens another"[3] and "The heartfelt counsel of a friend is as sweet as perfume and incense."[4] They value the candor of a friend who is willing to "speak the truth in love"[5] because they know how much it can help.

Our imperfections, shortcomings, and blind spots all remind us that we need trusted people in our lives who will give us constructive, honest, and loving feedback. Our personal growth, emotional health, and spiritual maturity all require healthy, constructive input from others. This kind of input can be of supreme value in making an engagement decision.

CHECK IN WITH THOSE WHO KNOW YOU BEST

Before you get engaged, I'd strongly suggest you consult with those who know you and your dating relationship best. Usually this means your family and friends. Find an appropriate time to sit down with them and share what you're thinking. Open up your heart and say something like, "Katie and I are at a place in our relationship where we are thinking about getting engaged. Since you know us best, I'd like to know what you think. From what you know about us and our relationship, do you think we should get married?" I think asking your family or friends a question like that is one of the wisest things you can do.

Before Bernice and I got engaged, I checked the pulse of my parents. Actually, like most sons and daughters, I already had a pretty good read on how they felt about Bernice. She made their heart beat fast. They liked her a lot. They definitely thought she would be good for me.

We all know that our parents have a way of giving us input about those we date, even without our asking. My parents made their support of Bernice obvious from day one. Whereas other girls I had dated or wanted to date got a big *thumbs down* from my parents, Bernice, from the moment we started dating, was given two *thumbs up*. It was pretty clear how they felt about her, and they would frequently suggest she'd make a great wife. The fact is, I never even had to ask them.

Even still, I wanted to be sure. So I checked in with my closest colleague. Jim Liljegren and I knew each other really well. We both worked together as full-time staff members at the same church. He was the music pastor. I was the youth director. We had spent countless hours together in meetings, lunches, and retreats. You name it, Jim knew me inside and out.

Jim also knew Bernice well. Besides the fact that she was often with me when I was with Jim, she had also been in his high school and college youth choirs. Jim had observed Bernice in numerous choir practices, prayer times, choir performances, and tough choir tour situations that included less-than-desirable conditions. Jim knew Bernice's heart and had seen her lifestyle up close.

The day I walked into Jim's office to get his read on my relationship with Bernice, I knew I could trust his counsel. Jim not only knew us well, he also had the wisdom of experience. At the time, Jim had already been married for eight years. That, plus the fact that he was older than me by ten years, gave me confidence in whatever advice he'd give.

I'll never forget Jim's reply when I asked him if he thought I should marry Bernice. "Dave," he said, "if you don't ask her, you'd be foolish. I think you'd make a great couple. What are you waiting for?"

Jim's support was very important to me. If he had said no, or if he'd had concerns, I doubt I would have gone through with getting engaged.

◉ BRENT

Over the past few years, I have become convinced that seeking an outside opinion is really important. I first realized that as I watched the engagement process of my friends.

My friend Paul got engaged without consulting me or anyone

else he hung out with. If he had asked me if I thought they should get married, I don't know what I would have said. That's a tough position that I didn't have to deal with because he didn't ask.

Why didn't Paul ask? I think he already knew what my answer would be and didn't want to hear it. He just wanted to be happy, not honest. Not surprisingly, Paul didn't involve many of us in the preparation for their wedding either. Their relationship often seemed to be hidden from us. I'm praying that things will work out for them in the long run, but I'm worried.

In contrast, my friend Rick made sure to ask us, his closest friends, if we thought he should marry his lovely girlfriend Betty. We all were unanimously supportive and encouraging, and I think this knowledge helped reaffirm what they already knew—they were good together. The wedding and wedding preparation were better, too, because of their openness and involvement of others in the process. Their relationship felt honest and had a peace surrounding it.

I want to have an honest relationship that is surrounded by peaceful support. Therefore, I'm doing my best to involve others in the process of considering engagement with Danielle. I'll admit, it's easy to get in my own little world with Danielle and think everything is great. But I know it's better to get an outside opinion.

If you're not willing to involve others, maybe it's because you already know what they're going to say, and you just don't want to hear it. Think about it.

YOUR PARENTS' INPUT MAY
SAVE YOU FROM A LOT OF PAIN

It's not that your parents and friends have a corner on wise counsel. It's just that they may see things in your life or your relationship that may be out of sight to you. Blind spots, remember?

Just last week Bernice and I had lunch with some parents who are still living through the painful aftermath of their oldest son's divorce. As we sat and listened to them, I couldn't help but think how important it is to get and heed the advice of those closest to you before you get engaged.

We asked them to tell us their son's story. Sharon said, "Our son Tom was such a model child. All through high school, he was the kid that all the parents of the kids in the youth group trusted. His winsome personality, confidence, and independent personality were assets growing up."

"Sounds like you have a great son," I said, "the kind of guy that a lot of girls would love to date. Tell me about Jan. How would you describe her?"

Tom's dad replied, "At first, when Tom started going out with Jan, we were delighted, because she came from a Christian home. In fact, we were best friends with her parents. Our families had known each other since she was a little child. But a few months before they got engaged, we started to notice that their relationship was not what we had expected. Tom and Jan didn't put the other person first. They spoke to each other with subtle put-downs."

At that point Sharon jumped back into the conversation and said, "Soon Tom was trying to impress her with material things that he couldn't afford. We knew Jan came from a very wealthy family, and that seemed to impress Tom. But it also put him under great pressure. Those areas and more gave us strong reservations about the two of them marrying."

I asked if Tom had asked them how they felt before he got engaged, or if they had expressed their reservations to him.

Sharon replied, "We tried a few times to get Tom to talk about their relationship, but each time we tried to talk to him about it, he withdrew. So, although we prayed, we didn't have those heart-to-heart talks that might have made a difference. If we could do things over again or give advice to others, we wouldn't just initiate the conversations before the wedding. We would have built into our relationship with Tom far more *courageous conversations* throughout the years, to prepare us to really help him in his most important decisions."

"Yeah," Bill added, "we firmly believe that if Tom and Jan had stepped back from the marriage, gotten counseling before the marriage, and worked through some of their major differences, the outcome would not have been the tragedy that it was."

As it turned out, Tom and Jan divorced three years after they married.

NOT ALL COUNSEL HAS EQUAL VALUE

I'd be one of the first to say that not all of the counsel you may get from your friends, your parents, or others will always be right. If you think back to the three stories I told in chapter ten, behind each one of those stories was mixed counsel.

If Mark had listened to his family and friends sooner, he certainly would never have bought the engagement ring, and most likely he would have ended the relationship months earlier. When Mark told me about his lack of peace and his ultimate breakup with Kim, he added, "I ignored the counsel and feelings of my family and friends. Both Mom and Dad never had good feelings about our relationship. But instead of listening to them, I chose to defend Kim's and my relationship. Now I know that was dumb."

Remember Kathy and Bob? Everyone they knew gave them green-light input. In fact, their counselors went so far as to pull the "I've heard from God on this one" card. They adamantly said, "You need to get married." Today Kathy and Bob are thanking

God that they had the nerve to ignore their counselors' counsel and their friends' and family's green-light support. Had they not done that, they may have made Greg and Becky's mistake.

Do you recall that even I, when it came to giving input to my own brother, didn't give wise counsel? Granted, it was at the last minute, and since I lived two hundred and fifty miles away and didn't really know much about Greg and Becky's relationship, I thought he was just getting pre-wedding cold feet. But the bottom line was, even I didn't see the red flag that was waving right in front of my face. My "no, Greg, you're just nervous; everything will be fine" words were very unwise.

YOU MUST MAKE THE FINAL CALL

In the final analysis, you are going to need to take all the counsel you receive and carefully sift it. Weigh it. Does it have merit? How does it fit with all the other things we're talking about in this book? You need to ask yourself questions like these:

- Are they giving me a green, yellow, or red flag?
- Do I agree with what others are saying and seeing?
- Is there merit to what is being said?
- How does their advice line up with other preengagement factors?
- How should I respond?

Keep the following two biblical principles in mind. First, *you need others' input.* Those who don't get wise input aren't as wise as they think they are. As Isaiah said, "Woe to those who are wise in their own eyes and clever in their own sight."[6] Humble yourself, restrain your pride, and open your heart and ears to what the significant others in your life are saying and thinking.

Second, *you need to carefully weigh others' input before you act.* What you hear may or may not be right for you. Remember these words: "A simple man believes anything, but a prudent man gives thought to his steps."[7] Before you jump in, hook, line, and sinker, carefully check out the validity of what you've been told.

◗ BRENT

For me it's important to remember that seeking the opinion of others is a very good idea, but the outside input will likely only answer the question of *should* we; it won't necessarily answer the question of *when.* I say this because it's a big lesson that Danielle and I learned.

BRENT: Hi, Danielle.

DANIELLE: Hi, Brent. Another interview for the book?

BRENT: Last one, I promise.

DANIELLE: OK, it better be. These people are going to know everything about us.

BRENT: Yes, it's the last one, and yes they know everything. Too bad for us.

DANIELLE: [Laughs] What's the question?

BRENT: When you told your parents we were thinking about getting married, what happened?

DANIELLE: Well, as you know, my parents got engaged two months into their relationship. Granted, they knew each other much longer than you and I did. Still, they were aware that wise people could decide in a short amount of time to marry each other, and still have a good marriage. (They are still happily married.) I was very precise with the type of man I was interested in, and they were aware of this. When they met you (note to readers: the "you" I refer to is Brent, not actually you the reader. That would just be silly!), they saw how well we aligned in personality, goals, and lifestyle. They fully supported our getting married in the next year.

BRENT: When you told your friends we were thinking about getting married, what happened?

DANIELLE: The opposite. While my parents were excited, my friends were a bit more worried about me emotionally and spiritually, because they knew my past relationships in the "boy area" a little better. They had also seen too many young couples rushing into marriage to fulfill what our college refers to as the "ring by spring" goal. They were nice and cordial, because they had to be. In all reality, I don't think they knew what to say about it, because I didn't really display the "I'm receptive to your opinion" mentality. They liked you, but it's not exactly easy to have one's close friend just decide one day that she's going to marry someone and ask no questions. Furthermore, it was harder for them to get to know you with such a large expectation already in their minds. Basically, they were worried that I was moving too fast.

BRENT: Want to share anything about how this affected your thinking and your relationship with them?

DANIELLE: I think I used my parents' experience as an excuse to follow my own agenda with us, while my friends sat in silence, unsure of what to do about the denial I was in. For me, making a quick decision about marriage was easier than thinking it through. But ultimately, I wasn't ready to make a decision at all. Since then, I have been able to see that neither my parents nor friends had the answer, but they were a healthy "check" for me. And I'm learning to find that healthy balance between knowing myself and making a decision for myself, while acknowledging that what others say is meaningful, necessary, and crucial in my relationships with those I care about.

BRENT: Well put. Well put. What a sharp girl.
DANIELLE: Yes, I know.

> So I really think it's important to do two things in this process:
> 1. Ask and be honest. Don't be afraid to involve others or to be honest with yourself. If you're not going to be honest or really take into account what someone tells you, then you may want to read this book again. I'd assume most are like me, though, and want to be honest and want to make the right choice. In that case . . .
> 2. Make the final call. Remember that people aren't perfect and their answers aren't necessarily perfect, but they are always revealing and can be extremely helpful as you work toward making a wise decision.

Before I wrote this book, I surveyed a hundred married couples and asked them about their engagement experiences. One of the questions I asked them was, "What suggestions would you give to couples who want to be sure they should get married?" The answers I received to this question were pretty much in line with what I've shared with you in this book.:

- Pay attention to your personal well-being.
- Make sure you're ready to make an unconditional commitment for life.
- Check your values—do they align?
- Be in love.
- Make sure you have healthy communication.
- Be sure that you make a good team.

I hope that by now you agree with their suggestions and the other areas I've addressed in this book.

While all of these issues are vital, I found that the two areas that got the most attention in their answers focused on getting a green light from God, your family, and your friends. Most echoed the sentiments of this person, who wrote, "We don't know ourselves clearly sometimes. We are too emotionally involved. Ask family members or close friends who knew you before and during your relationship for their honest opinion. Be willing to hear the answer, even if it's not what you wanted to hear."[8] That pretty much summarizes what I've been trying to say in this chapter.

❷ BRENT'S FINAL THOUGHTS

Well, this is it. No more entries from me. The last section of the book is going to be about what you do once you've answered the "should we get engaged?" question with a yes, no, or maybe. I'll let my dad handle that section alone.

For me, the process of going through this book has been extremely helpful. Over the months it took to write, I learned so much, both personally and in my relationship with Danielle.

What's that? You want to know what I've decided about marrying Danielle? I bet you would. Will I ask her soon? Will we wait? Will we end things? If I told you, then that would be cheating. I'm sorry, but I just can't share that information yet. First, I should probably talk it over with Danielle before I tell you. Second, I can't give you an answer yet about what's supposed to happen. I'm sure our journey has been very different from that of many who are reading this, but I hope that somehow it has provided a helpful perspective in your processing.

Although I won't give a final answer, I will say that in writing my parts of this book, I have learned how important it is to:

- make sure God is the source of my fulfillment and identity, not Danielle;

- learn to trust God with these decisions;
- be honest with myself and Danielle about where we're at; and
- avoid rushing things.

As long as I'm doing those things, I can embrace and enjoy what God has in store for me. And that is a wonderfully peaceful thing.

● DANIELLE'S FINAL THOUGHTS

My last chance to tell about my experience. Wow. What to say? For me, it has been all about the deeper, internal issues in my life. My fear of what my parents might say was rooted in my inability to trust myself. My fear of what my friends would say was rooted in what they might do (e.g., abandon me because I was getting married, think I was a weirdo, tell me what to do—a lot of irrational fears that actually had to do with my past friendships).

I'm about to graduate from college, so my mind goes "every which way" a little too often. Making decisions about the rest of my life doesn't feel very easy, especially when it's such a new experience. It's been really important for me to get to know myself and trust that God will lead me on His way.

Brent has taught me a lot about this. Today (the day I write this) hasn't been the only time Brent's said, "Danielle, just relax. You don't have to make a decision about this part of your life right now."

So, I'm resting on the knowledge that my life is in service to God, my heart is filled with His mercy, and my source is Him. From there, I'm just hoping that God will work everything out and that His path for Brent and me will be clear.

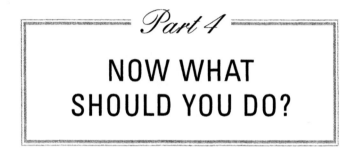

Part 4

NOW WHAT
SHOULD YOU DO?

Thirteen

● NEEDING TO GIVE
IT MORE TIME

𝒞 aptain Howard Peterson knew his career was over after he landed his Southwest Airlines 737-300 too fast at the Hollywood-Burbank Airport. Fortunately no one was killed after the jet crashed through a fence at the end of the runway and skidded into a nearby gas station.

The whole March 5, 2000, accident could have been avoided if Captain Peterson had only performed the mandated safety checks and not ignored the series of warning horns and sirens that sounded for thirty-five seconds before the landing. He even brushed off a mechanized voice just before landing that was telling him to pull up. Howard chose to ignore that, too, and simply said, "That's all right."

Well, it wasn't all right. The fully loaded 737-300 came in at 209 miles per hour, well above the maximum landing speed of 160 miles per hour. He couldn't get the airplane to stop in time. The jet crashed through the fence at the end of the runway. Then Captain Peterson remorsefully said, "My fault. My fault . . . Well, there goes my career."[1] He was right about that!

Talk about a bad decision. A plane was lost. A career was ended. Passengers were shaken up. Some sustained physical injures. Others are now living with lifelong emotional scars.

When it comes right down to it, the whole mess could have been avoided if Captain Peterson had only paid attention to the safety limits and blaring alarms. Everyone would have been much better off if he had only heeded the signs and backed off. Yes, it would have taken a little more time to pull up, circle the airport, perform all of the mandatory safety checks, and then slow the jet down and land at a safe speed. But just a few extra minutes would have prevented a major amount of damage. If he had been safe, he wouldn't have ended up sorry.

As this book comes to a close, like Captain Peterson, you may be faced with a dangerous landing. For you that means getting engaged. You may be hearing warning signals going off all around you. They may be blaring and glaring in your relationship and in your heart. You may be able to see and hear them clearly, or you may just detect a quiet whisper telling you this may not be right—that this is not what's best for you.

So now you're faced with a very important decision. Will you ignore what you can see and feel, or will you back off, take some more time, and make sure everything is right before you go ahead and get engaged?

IF YOU DOUBT, DON'T!

Let me introduce you to a very important biblical principle that may fit your situation. *If you have doubts—don't do it.* The Bible says that if you're thinking about doing something about which you have doubts, *don't do it.* Your doubts may be God's warning signal to protect you from making a big mistake. Back off. Take some more time. Rethink what you're about to do. A doubt may be God's way of keeping you, or someone you care about, out of harm's way and the inevitable hurtful consequences that could come.

My thinking about doubts is connected to two biblical passages. The first is Paul's answer to the Christians in Rome, who were in a quandary about whether or not they should be eating meat that may have been offered to an idol. Some of these believers had no problem eating this kind of meat. To them, an idol was nothing more than a man-made object. It wasn't God. It wasn't even a little "g" god. It was nothing more than a piece of wood. Therefore, meat offered to nothing meant nothing was wrong with the meat. "So eat up and enjoy it!" they said.

Others in Rome saw the same issue differently. They weren't so sure you could just eat up and enjoy it. Their minds and hearts told them it was wrong to eat meat that had been offered to an idol. Their viewpoint gave them strong feelings of doubt. To these Christ followers Paul said, "The man who has doubts is condemned if he eats, because his eating is not from faith; and everything that does not come from faith is sin."[2] If you have doubts—don't! It may look good, it may taste good, but it won't be good if you can't eat it free of doubts. Even though it may have been only a small serving of meat, it wasn't a minor issue to just brush aside. It would actually be a sin for them to go ahead and eat. Eating would be the wrong thing to do.

Now I'm not saying it would be a sin to get engaged if you have doubts about it. But I am suggesting the principle applies. *If you have doubts—don't.*

James, the Lord's brother, spoke to the problem of praying with doubts. James said, "When he asks, he must believe and not doubt, because he who doubts is like a wave of the sea, blown and tossed by the wind. That man should not think he will receive anything from the Lord."[3]

If you doubt—don't! Don't waste your breath praying, because your prayers are going to do no good. If you can't believe God can give you the wisdom you need, don't bother asking. He only gives needed wisdom to those who believe He can. You're better asking God to first give you faith to believe that He can answer your prayers.

If you doubt—don't. Don't eat meat. Don't bother to pray. And I'd add, *don't get engaged.* In my thinking, if God doesn't want someone with doubts doing something as mundane as eating meat or as essential as praying, I don't think He would recommend that you get engaged if you're having doubts. I'm talking about real doubts. Doubts that have you thinking you're making a mistake:

- *I am not sure if I should go through with this.*
- *This could be the wrong person.*
- *I don't think I am ready for this.*

I think God would say if you're having those kind of doubts, *don't.* Don't pop the question yet. Don't say yes if he asks you to marry him. Don't force it. Back off. Take some time to evaluate why you're feeling this way. Find out what's going on. Regroup.

Get perspective. Take whatever time you need individually or as a couple to get to the bottom of what your doubts mean.

Whatever you do, don't ignore the doubts that are in your mind and the yellow lights that are in your relationship. Don't get engaged until you are sure you're doing the right thing. Let Paul and Barbara's experience help you determine to resolve your doubts before you get engaged.

NOT READY YET

Paul was twenty-five and Barbara was twenty-one when they first met and began dating. Their love for each other grew rapidly and they began to think about the possibility of getting married. When that desire reached a fever peak with Paul, he popped the question—prematurely. That became obvious when Barbara asked her parents for permission to marry Paul.

"Before I can give Paul permission to marry you," Barbara's dad said, "I'd like him to do a few things. First, he needs to finish college. Then he needs to get a job and find a place to live. If he'll do these things first, I will give you my support."

"That's where I got off the wagon," Paul told me. "After her parents asked Barbara to tell me to do those things, I said to myself, 'I don't need this.' So I called the whole thing off. Barbara and I got unengaged."

"Did you agree with her parents?" I asked.

"Yeah, they were right. But I didn't like them telling me what to do through Barbara. If they had told me to my face, maybe it would have been different. Either way, I wasn't ready. They knew it, and I knew it too."

"So you knew you weren't ready?" I asked.

"Yes," Paul replied, "it really came down to this. I loved Barbara—I cared for her a lot—but I cared for me a lot more.

Actually I was in love with somebody else. It was *me*! Plus, on top of my self-love issues were some underlying doubts. I really was beginning to question whether or not I wanted to give up my freedom as a single. I still liked doing my own thing. I hadn't stopped looking at other girls. I wasn't sure I wanted to be tied down to one person."

"Did Barbara have similar feelings?" I asked.

"No, not really, at least not at first," Paul replied. "It was more my problem. I was the one still struggling. But my issues soon became an issue between us. Then even Barbara started having doubts."

"What do you mean?" I asked.

"After our very, very short, unapproved engagement," Paul said, "we went back to just seeing each other from time to time. We decided to not officially date. That went on for a while, but then we got to a point where we decided we wanted to try to be boyfriend and girlfriend again. That worked great, and we kept trying to intentionally sort this thing out. That went on for the next two years.

"Two years," I replied. "That's a long time to still hold out hope, isn't it?"

"Yes, but those two years were really important. I changed a lot, and so did our relationship. I started to seriously address my selfishness issues. We as a couple grew closer. Once again, we started to hope that our relationship would end up in marriage. When it seemed like we were getting there, I even went out and bought an engagement ring. I was planning to give the ring to Barbara on her birthday."

"So it was on her birthday when you proposed a second time?"

"No, it actually came two weeks after that. I probably would have asked Barbara to marry me on her birthday, but when that day came, she got ahead of me. She said, 'Paul, today would sure be a special day to get an engagement ring.' When she said that, it made me not want to ask her. So I didn't. Even after all that time, I still didn't want anyone even indirectly telling me what and when to do something. It was just another sign that I still wasn't ready. But two weeks later, on my own time, I decided the time was right, so I asked her to marry me."

"And this time what did she say?" I asked Paul.

"She said no," Paul replied.

"No! I thought she wanted to marry you—that she was looking forward to getting a ring?"

"She was," Paul replied, "but my lack of sensitivity in our relationship over the two weeks following her birthday just added more fuel to her own doubts. So it was like we needed more time or something. As it turned out, we needed a lot more time."

ALMOST BACK TO SQUARE ONE

Over the next eight months, Paul and Barbara went back to just being friends again. They took more time to work on their own personal issues and to seek an answer to where their relationship should go. Those months apart were also very important for Paul. His relationship with God grew, as did his willingness to make an unconditional love commitment to Barbara—if they ever got back together again.

After what seemed like another eternity apart, Paul met Barbara for coffee. They talked about how each had been and how things were going. Then Paul told her what he had been thinking for months. He said, "Barbara, I've come to a point where I know for sure I love you and want to marry you. I want to have an exclusive one-woman relationship with you and you alone. Would you like to get engaged to be married?"

"So that's how it happened," I said.

"Well yes and no." Paul said. "Yes is what I said, and no is what she said—at least for the next three months."

Barbara's response to Paul's proposal was, "Next week I am going to be leaving on a three-month trip with my girlfriends to Europe. While I am gone, I will think about your proposal. After all we've been through, I'm just not sure. When I get back, I'll let you know."

OK, I'M FINALLY SURE

Paul had another three months to be sure as he waited and prayed. So did Barbara. And when Barbara got back from her trip, she met Paul with an absolute yes. Both were finally sure. Their doubts and reservations were finally in the past.

At this point, even Barbara's parents added their support. Of course, by now six years had passed and Paul had finished college. He had a job. He had a place to live. And he was even attending seminary. Paul and Barbara were married eight months later.

From the time they had met to the time they were engaged, it took eight years. But those eight years were worth it. During that time, each grew and changed. They built a strong foundation for their relationship. They entered into engagement and marriage convinced they were doing the right thing.

YOU NEED TO BE SURE

I have good news for you. It usually doesn't happen that way. Eight years is way too long for most couples to keep trying to make a relationship work. But however long it takes, it's vital that you take whatever time is needed to be sure. Paul and Barbara did the right thing by not going through with engagement and marriage until they knew for sure. Like them, you want to be personally, relationally, and spiritually sure.

If you have serious doubts, don't ignore them. Get to the bottom of them. Trent and Jan wish now they had done that. They, like Captain Peterson, ignored them, and now they are sorry for it. Here's a portion of a letter Jan recently sent me:

> Hi, Pastor Dave,
>
> My husband and I have been counseling with Pastor Stan, and things are not looking at all good for us. As you may verify with him if you wish, we jumped a lot of steps and rushed into marriage after a short four-month courtship, feeling that as mature adults we knew what we were looking for.
>
> Since we were married, however, I have spent plenty of time reflecting on the mistake we made. From the start, we shoved aside our doubts with thoughts of "it will all work out" and rushed headlong into marriage. We just dated for a short while and started talking about marriage . . . way too soon. I am now paying the price for this hasty and poorly thought-out decision. If we would have only taken the time to have dealt with our doubts and other issues, we would have spared ourselves a lot of pain.
>
> Well, now Trent has moved on, and I don't know what the future will hold for us. Please keep us in your prayers . . .

If you're having doubts about your readiness to get engaged—for whatever reasons—do yourself a big favor. Don't ignore them. Get to the bottom of what's giving you doubts. Wait. Take whatever time you need. Just do the very best you can to be sure before you take the next step.

Fourteen

● HOW TO GRACIOUSLY MOVE ON

$\mathcal{F}$or over a year our daughter Katie put off the inevitable. She kept hoping and praying that her problem would just go away all by itself. She hoped she wouldn't have to deal with it—that the pain would just disappear. It didn't. And when the pain got so bad she could hardly stand it any longer, she finally decided it was time to do something about it.

Katie had a number of plantar warts on the bottom of her feet. I know—gross. And painful. She tried all the "easy" treatments, but none of them worked. She tried to just ignore them. She tried to just live with the pain. She finally decided to get help. When the pain was too much for her to endure any longer, it pushed her to do what she didn't want to do—she had to let the doctor cut them out.

I was with Katie when the doctor surgically removed the warts. It was awful. It was painful. I know that because she verbally let us know! But she toughed it out because she knew the long-term benefits would far outweigh the immediate pain. And it has. Her feet are back to normal. She has a few minor scars, but they are nothing in comparison to the pain she had lived with. She is so much better off now than she was before.

Katie has only one regret: she wishes she hadn't waited so long to take care of the problem. She realizes now that she didn't have to live with the pain for as long as she did. But her reluctance to have the warts cut out was understandable, especially when the doctor had told her, "There is nothing more painful than having surgery on the bottom of your feet. The surgery itself hurts like crazy. And your recovery will be painful and slow."

MAKING THE TOUGH CALL

If you're in a serious relationship in which everyone is assuming you're heading toward engagement and marriage, but you know there are serious problems, you can probably identify with Katie. You may be saying, "I know there's a problem here, but I don't want to have to deal with it. It will be easier to just ride it out. Maybe it will get better on its own."

You'd like the problem to just go away all by itself. You don't want to hurt anyone. You just want everything to be OK. But the fact is, the problems aren't going to just go away, any more than Katie's warts were going to just disappear on their own. You have to face the issue head-on if you want to ultimately end up in a healthy and happy marriage.

Years ago King Solomon said, "There is a time for everything, and a season for every activity under heaven."[1] He included in the time for everything "a time to plant and a time to uproot . . .

a time to embrace and a time to refrain . . . a time to search and a time to give up . . . a time to be silent and a time to speak."[2]

Wise words. Life includes hard times and easy times. It will have its share of good times and bad times. We may wish life were one big good time, but that's just not the way it is this side of heaven.

When we apply this truth to dating relationships, it's clear that singles will experience relational beginnings and endings. In some cases, a relationship may end up lasting for a lifetime—till *death do us part*; in other cases, it may be rather short-lived—till *differences drive you apart*.

This principle also suggests that within dating relationships couples will experience:

- times when a hug and kiss are all that's needed to patch things up;
- times when some serious issues need to be dealt with together before the relationship can move on; and
- quiet, contemplative times of listening or thinking. If the conclusions drawn suggest a future separation, you must find a way to express that truth in a way that will be good for you and the one you've cared deeply about.

WE HAD SO MUCH GOING FOR US, BUT . . .

Walt and Sherri can identify with Solomon's thoughtful insights. Their twenty-first-century relationship, which began with so much promise, eventually fell apart, and now they are living in the aftermath.

When Walt and Sherri met online at eharmony.com, it looked as if they were a perfect match. They both felt they might have found the person they had been searching for. Walt said, "It would be safe to say that I perceived our relationship moving toward engagement and marriage."

Who wouldn't, when you have as much in common as Walt and Sherri did? Their values and career aspirations matched up. Both enjoyed mountain biking. Their open communication was rock solid. Their shared spiritual beliefs were a frequent topic in their conversations and prayers. Several times a week they did something a lot of couples never do: they prayed together!

With Walt at twenty-seven years old, and Sherri at thirty, each was more than ready to be done with the single life. They would have loved for this relationship to have been their last dating relationship, but it didn't work out that way.

With their relationship seeming to be so perfect, I asked Walt what happened. Were there yellow flags?

Walt replied, "I'm not sure there were yellow flags per se, but rather a sense that the road ahead was one that should be traveled with caution, and thus required prayerful preparation. In simple terms, we had gotten to know each other well enough and spent enough time together to reach the point where we needed to evaluate whether our relationship would continue to progress and get more serious or if it was time to seek a different direction. We both agreed that long-term dating with no goal or development was not part of God's will for us."

"In other words," I replied, "you guys didn't want to keep dating if your dating wasn't going to ultimately lead you to marriage. Is that what you mean?"

"Yes," Walt replied. "It was more of a direction, goal, and motivation question. Where was our relationship going? What did we both hope it would achieve? Based on these questions, why should or shouldn't our relationship continue?"

I said, "So up to this point in time, you had a great relationship. At least you thought you did. But you were uncertain about the future. You weren't sure if you were moving toward marriage or not."

"Yes," Walt said. "That's pretty much it."

"So what did you do to get an answer to your unsettled feelings?" I asked.

"We prayed," Walt said. "We agreed to have a time of intense prayer and reflection apart, and then we talked and compared notes."

STOP, THINK, AND PRAY

I can really identify with Walt and Sherri's prayer response. A few years ago Bernice and I came to a similar place in our lives. Our confusion, however, concerned the next step in my career. At the time I was considering an offer to become the senior pastor at a church in Santa Barbara, California.

Bernice and I both love Santa Barbara—a lot! We'd both lived in this beautiful coastal city for two years during college. Since then we'd longed to go back and live there again. The outstanding weather and beach city life is our idea of heaven on earth. That's why we were ready to jump at the chance to move there when this church asked me if I was ready to be an official candidate for the senior pastor position.

The process a pastor and a church go through during this "candidating" time is very similar to what two people go through who are engaged and preparing for marriage. As in a relationship, "engagement" to a church is a huge decision. It means you both are ready to take steps toward marriage. If "marriage" is when the congregation and a new pastor say, "I do" to each other, "engagement" is when you say, "OK, I'd love to be your pastor. Let's take whatever steps are necessary to confirm that decision and make it happen."

Our love for Santa Barbara, the opportunity for ministry with some great people, the fact that we'd still be fairly close to our two older children, and the financial offer all made this possibility very appealing. I wanted to jump in and say yes. But Bernice and I were both unsure. We didn't have complete peace. We needed to sort out our strong *this would be great* feelings from the reality of the church situation and whether or not this would really be the right thing to do. Bernice and I, like Walt and Sherri, were at a crossroads. So we did the same thing Walt and Sherri did. We set aside a time for intense prayer to seek God's will and ask for His clear direction.

For us, that meant a twelve-hour period of time when we agreed to fast and pray and journal our thoughts and feelings apart from each other. Then we came back together to share what we felt should be our next step. At the end of that time, we both felt God's answer was no. Neither of us wanted it to be no! But as much as we would have loved to live and minister in Santa Barbara, both of us knew it just wasn't right for us, and we needed to call it off. Two hours after I called the church in Santa Barbara and gave them our answer, God opened a totally unexpected door. But that's another story.

DECIDING NOT TO GO ON

After Walt and Sherri's weekend apart to pray, they, too, reached an answer. In their case, however, it was different. "For us," Walt said, "we came to different conclusions. I thought things should move forward, but she felt that God was not leading her in that direction. At the time, this was obviously very tough for me to swallow, but eventually I came to accept that if engagement and marriage had been part of God's plan for us, He would have worked in Sherri's heart toward that purpose. In the immediate aftermath of our breakup, I struggled with a lot of pain and hurt. I even flirted with the idea that somehow Sherri was being stubborn and messing up God's plan. However, I came to realize the folly of this idea. No human was going to thwart God's perfect plan for me, so I had to move on and look forward to what He would do next."

Shortly after Walt and Sherri had that difficult conversation, Walt wrote me this letter:

Pastor Dave,

I am very sorry to say that it does not look like things with Sherri and me will be moving forward. We had a very long conversation tonight, and she expressed that she has deep-seated doubts and uncertainties that she just cannot shake. She said wonderful things about me and indicated that I had treated her better than she could have hoped for, but that in her heart, she just could not see things moving forward. There were a lot of tears shed from both of us, but there wasn't any way to argue about it. We shared a very tearful prayer, where we both asked God to bless the other and to bring the right person into their life.

It is a hard thing to swallow and challenges me in very deep places. However, I do trust that God has a plan for my life and that in time He will reveal it to me . . . I appreciate your prayers and support.

Walt

PICKING UP THE PIECES

Real life. Real pain. Crushed hopes. Shattered dreams. I asked Walt later how it had gone as he gradually picked up the pieces and moved on.

Walt replied, "It was very hard. The toughest part was some-how reframing and rethinking my goals and hopes. Once a per-son has started to think about a future that always includes someone else, it is very difficult to suddenly face a future that doesn't involve that person, at least not in the capacity you had envisioned."

I really understand that. When you think you have some-thing special, so special that it might lead to marriage, and it doesn't, it's going to hurt. In fact, the only way to take pain out of these kinds of times in life is to take love out of life. If you hadn't loved each other, the pain wouldn't be so great. But when you love someone deeply and share a deep relational, emotional, and spiritual connection, and then have that con-nection broken, it's going to hurt.

If it's possible that you are headed for this kind of hurt, I'd love to remove it from your future. Of course, you and I both know that ignoring the problem and pretending that everything will work out is an unwise thing to do. If you think the pain of ending the relationship is going to hurt now, be assured that the longer you wait, the more painful it will be.

Yes, breaking off a relationship that you thought was head-ing toward engagement and marriage will hurt. But breaking off an engagement—especially as you get closer and closer to the wedding—will be even more painful, and the pain will affect even more people.

And of course, getting married and then divorced would bring pain and consequences that will stay with you and your families and possibly your children for the rest of your lives. You will be much better off dealing with it as soon as possible, so that you can both get on to a better future.

BE VERY, VERY CAREFUL

How you go about breaking off the relationship is important. The words *carefully* and *tenderly* are appropriate here. If you, like Sherri, feel that things aren't working out, I urge you to turn to God in prayer. This is the first important step toward finding peace and direction. Ask for God's help.

God invites you, as He invited Jeremiah the prophet, to pray when you don't know what to do. He says, "Call to me and I will answer you and tell you great and unsearchable things you do not know."[3]

Set time aside to pray and seek God's will. I believe if you are serious about seeking God's will in this way, He will reveal it to you. I've found that Bible reading and journaling are also helpful as you contemplate your next step. Write down your thoughts and feelings. It will help you sort out what to do next.

If you ultimately decide you need to break up and move on with your life, ask God to help you do it *tenderly*. This isn't the time for harsh, hurtful words. Break the news in a respectful, loving way. The goal is to move out of a dating relationship into a friendship. How you do that is important.

When Walt described how Sherrie broke things off with him, and the way it could happen to others, he said, "First, they would be lucky to have someone like Sherri who had nothing but good things to say about me. In fact, she even prayed that God would bring the right woman into my life. I am not sure you can be angry or harbor any ill feelings when someone does that!"

Walt went on to say, "During the weeks after we broke up, she even sent me several e-mails to check on me and let me know that she was praying for God to grant me peace and acceptance."

God has done that. Walt and Sherri are still friends. Each still cares about the other and wishes nothing but the best for each other. Both are grateful that she did what she needed to do. Sherrie made the tough call, and today they are both better off for it.

What Walt didn't expect was what he's enjoying now—life with a new girlfriend. He doesn't know yet what the future holds for the two of them. For now he's just glad to live one day at a time knowing that God's plan is perfect and he can trust Him for whatever's up ahead.

Fifteen

● READY TO POP THE QUESTION

$\mathcal{N}$ ASCAR fans live for the green flag. It means the wait is finally over. When the green flag drops and a National Association for Stock Car Auto Racing event begins, ecstatic fans standing all around the racetrack let loose and shout their support. Let the fun begin. Full speed ahead. The race has officially begun.

Engagement is a green flag. It's the culminating moment when a couple officially says, "Let's go. Let the race to marriage begin. We're ready to make a lifelong commitment to each other. We're sure this is the right thing to do."

If you've read through this book and applied the things you've learned, and you feel as if you're ready to get engaged, you've probably gone through a lot to get to this point.

Individually, you've carefully and in some cases tenaciously prepared yourself for this moment. You realize you're not perfect, but you're not a mess either. You can see signs of emotional and spiritual stability in your life. You've decided that you're ready to settle down with one person, and you believe you've found that person. You willingly want to make an unconditional commitment to be a husband, or wife, for life. You have considered the timing and feel it is the right time to move forward with marriage.

As a couple, you see signs that confirm you're right for each other. Your love for each other is genuine. Your values and faith are aligned. Your strong connection and complementary qualities make you a great team. Your heart is at peace. You don't see any yellow or red flags waving over your relationship.

Your readiness to marry—and to marry this particular person—has also been confirmed by others. Your friends, family, and faith in God are all telling you to *pop the question*. Not only do you feel you're right for each other, but those closest to you are saying the same thing.

Before every NASCAR race, crews are meticulous in their pre-race preparations. Crew chiefs know races are often won or lost due to how thoroughly a car is prepared before the race begins. The chances of winning are heightened when everything on the pre-race checklist checks out.

CHECKLIST CHECK

This book has basically been a preengagement checklist. It has given you twelve areas to closely examine before you pop the question. If at this point these areas have checked out, you should be able to answer the following questions with a strong yes:

1. Would you marry you?
2. Are you all dated out?
3. Are you ready to make a "till death do you part" commitment?
4. Is the timing right?
5. Are you genuinely "in love"?
6. Do you communicate effectively?
7. Are you on the same page?
8. Are you spiritually connected?
9. Are you better together than you are apart?
10. Is your heart at peace?
11. Do you believe this is God's will?
12. Are your friends and family supportive?

If these areas have all checked out, I am really excited for you. You're ready to take the next step. I love it when a couple comes to this point in their relationship. When each knows he or she has found *the one*. All the years of dreaming, hoping, thinking, waiting, and praying for this day are finally over.

READY TO POP THE QUESTION

Now only one question remains to be answered—one that you can't answer for yourself. From the guy's side it's, "If I ask her to marry me, will she say yes?" From the girl's side it's, "Will he ask me to marry him?"

Hopefully, if you've both worked through all the things you've read in this book, you'll have a pretty good idea of how those questions will be answered. But until they're actually asked and answered, you are in a state of *engagement anticipation*. You're ready to get engaged, but you're still waiting for it to actually happen. I can identify with that feeling. In the days leading up to the time when Bernice and I got engaged I felt like I might go crazy.

Even after more than thirty years of marriage, I can still remember the excitement I felt when I was ready to ask Bernice to marry me. Once I had made that decision, it was hard to think about anything else. I lived anticipating the moment when I would ask.

I could have easily just asked and gotten it over with, but I wanted to do something special. So I decided to wait for a month and ask her while we were away on a retreat with the college group from our church. At the time, we were both living in Fresno, California.

When you're in Fresno, you're nowhere. But you're just a couple hours from a lot of great places: San Francisco, Yosemite, Lake Tahoe, Los Angeles, and the ocean. I felt the wait would be worth it, because the retreat was going to be on the coast.

As you may remember, both Bernice and I love the ocean. What better place to ask her than on the beach? After I decided where I would pop the question, I then started thinking about how to do it. At the time, most of my closest friends were already married. I was pretty much going to be the last one among my peers to take the plunge. That meant I had previously heard their unique engagement stories.

One popped the question during a movie. He put the engagement ring in a box of Cracker Jack. When she pulled the prize out of the box, instead of a plastic fluorescent ring, she found a diamond engagement ring. That was a big hit for him, and it turned out to be a big disturbance for everyone else who was watching the movie. When he told me about his engagement, I thought, *That's pretty cool.*

Another friend used a box of See's candy to pop the question. He put the engagement ring in one of the little brown candy wraps. He said it was the sweetest way he could think of to ask her to marry him.

I realized that either of those options would work with Bernice, because she likes Cracker Jack and she loves See's candy. But I really wanted to have her pick out the rings with me, so I had to come up with another plan.

I ultimately decided to simply write Bernice a letter and give it to her at her favorite place—the beach. I'd love to share that letter with you, but I can't. It was mysteriously lost, which is too bad. It was probably the best letter I've ever written, because it revealed how much Bernice meant to me and how I wanted to spend the rest of my life with her.

Before Bernice and I went away for the beach retreat, I wrote and rewrote that letter until it said exactly what I wanted. Then I put it into my suitcase for safekeeping. The final twenty-four hours before I popped the question were excruciating. Talk about *engagement anticipation*. I had a full dose of it. In my book *Before You Live Together*,[1] I explain how the whole thing turned out.

> That night I did not sleep well. My adrenaline was running high. With my excitement about popping the big question, Saturday could not come soon enough.
>
> The next morning I awoke to a picture-perfect day. Bernice and I drove through Monterey. At one point, just as I had planned, we stopped at a beautiful spot overlooking the Pacific Ocean and I pulled out a letter that I had previously written. I told Bernice I had spent a lot of time thinking and praying about our relationship, and I wanted her to know how I felt. With that, I gave her the letter and asked her if she would read it. After she finished reading about my love for her and my desire to spend the rest of my life with her, I asked her if she would marry me. She said yes.[2]

Looking back, part of me is still amazed Bernice said yes. But boy, was I ever grateful. I knew that "a good woman is hard to find, and worth far more than diamonds."[3] That was exactly how I viewed Bernice. I had come to believe if you "find a good spouse, you find a good life—and even more: the favor of GOD!"[4] I felt so fortunate to have found Bernice, I was ecstatic. The day we got engaged was a very, very special day in our lives—as it will be for you too.

If you're ready to get engaged, I encourage you to make your engagement day special. Don't let this life-changing moment slip by as just another day. Of course, how and what this means is your call. Keep in mind, however you pop the question, it will be something you'll never forget.

As you consider what this may mean for you, it may be helpful to reflect on the four typical ways couples get engaged. Sometimes it happens through one of these ways; other times it happens in combination.

The Spur-of-the-Moment Proposal

Some couples end up getting engaged on the spur-of-the-moment. The groom-to-be can't wait any longer and just asks. Kind of like a shaken-up bottle of Coke that has its top popped off. In spite of their best intentions to make it special, some guys spill out their proposal when they can't hold it in any longer. That's how it happened for Bob.

After Bob dropped Kim off for an emergency dental appointment, he sped off to the jewelry store. While Kim was drugged and prepped for a root canal, Bob hurriedly bought the engagement ring both of them had previously looked at. His plan was to give it to her later that night while they were having dinner at a romantic restaurant.

After purchasing the ring, Bob made a beeline back to the

dental office, just in time to pick Kim up. As you can imagine, Kim was pretty much out of it when she came out. Her mouth was numb, which meant her speech was slurred, and she was pretty unstable on her feet. Bob ended up helping Kim walk out of the office and get into the car. He had left the ring sitting in a cute little box in the back seat.

As he and Kim approached the car, Bob's enthusiasm got the best of him. Instead of opening the front door, he opened the back door—so that Kim would see the box. Then after he was sure she saw it, he closed the back door, opened the front door, and helped Kim get in the car.

When Bob got in the car, Kim looked at him and was able to get out five slurred words: "Bob, what's in the box?" That's when Bob popped the question. Kim told me she slurred out the word *yes*. Since then, I've kidded Bob about his spur-of-the-moment proposal. I've told him that Kim might not have said yes if she hadn't been numb and on drugs. Which on second thought makes me think that his proposal may not have been so spur-of-the-moment after all.

A spur-of-the-moment proposal might work for you as it did for Bob and Kim. It wasn't very romantic, but it's a great story to tell the grandkids.

For some, just being with each other is enough to make the moment special. One woman said of her engagement, "There was really nothing special about it other than being with him. We actually got engaged in a parking lot, when we went out to the drugstore to run an errand for my mom."

The Well-Thought-Out Proposal

My proposal to Bernice was thought out, but not to the degree that some men will go. One wife told me the story of how when her husband proposed, he went to the effort to place twelve clues and twelve roses throughout their city. Each place he left a rose had special significance in their dating relationship.

One of the roses was left at the foot of the cross at a church they had gone to for a concert. That clue included a line from a favorite song the band had played that night, which had special meaning in their relationship. This couple's rose/clue hunt led up to a special time together, where he told her how much he loved her and then led her through several scriptures that focused on the joy of marriage. He led the two of them in prayer and then got down on one knee and proposed.

"His proposal was so special to me," another wife said to me, "because he put time, effort, and planning into it." This proposal began at a park on a Sunday after church with a picnic lunch that he had prepared. After they ate, he pulled out a scrapbook that he had put together. Picture after picture told their dating story. "As I turned the pages," this joyful wife said, "I came to a page that had a wedding invitation pasted on the center of the page. I opened it and it read, 'Let's spend the rest of our lives filling the remaining pages together . . . will you marry me?'" At that point he got down on one knee and presented her with a beautiful ring. Great plan. She loved it. She said yes!

The Special Place Proposal

A lot of proposals, like mine, are connected to a special place. That's how it was for Tim and Debbie. His proposal came after a special dinner at a favorite Italian restaurant that looked out over a lake. In this romantic setting, he was planning to pop the question after dinner, while the two of them went on a gondola ride around the lake. *This is going to be perfect*, Tim thought. The last time they had gone on this ride was the first time they had gone out together. "What better place to ask her to marry me?"

After dinner Tim and Debbie headed out for the gondola

ride, complete with a gondolier—which turned out to be a problem. Tim explained, "I was so excited to ask Debbie to marry me. I was ready and planning to ask her during our romantic gondola ride on the lake. But then I realized I couldn't do it. Not with a gondolier staring down my neck. He was about a foot away! Plus, I started to think that if I got down on one knee, I'd probably tip over the boat."

Tim did end up proposing that night at that special place— but just not on the boat. He waited until they got off, and then they walked around the lake to a beautiful little cove, where he knelt down on one knee and said, "I love you, I respect you, and I want to spend the rest of my life with you. Will you marry me?" Debbie said yes.

Your special place may be at a favorite restaurant or park or beach. Living in Phoenix, I know a lot of people who got engaged at the Grand Canyon. Some go to Niagara Falls. For one couple I know, it was at the zoo. Another couple got engaged on a roller coaster, just before it went over the top peak. He wanted to do it that way because that's where his grandparents got engaged, and their marriage had lasted more than sixty years. Plus, it was representative of all of the highs and lows they anticipated experiencing in their marital life ahead.

The Personal Touch Proposal

Most proposals include some kind of personal, special touch. For one wife-to-be, that meant a carrot cut into the shape of a diamond, because at that moment they couldn't afford a ring. For another couple who loved pizza, he put the ring on a pizza, which meant the ring had cheese and tomato sauce all over it. She later said, "It wasn't the best idea." But it was unique.

One husband I know used a poem he wrote. He titled his poem "All My Life."

All my life I've wondered who would be my wife
and what she would be like.
All my life I've wondered who would be
the mother of my children
and how we would learn together
to instill in them faith and discipline.
All my life I've wondered who would pray with me
and stay with me.
All my life I've wondered who would share my thoughts
and whose thoughts would be shared with me
to ensure deep and abiding intimacy.
All my life I've wondered who would
help me make a house a home
where others are always welcome.
Where our children can feel safe and secure.
Where memories can be created and then remembered again.
And where Christ can manifest His presence through us.
All my life I've wondered who would help me learn the
Dance of Love.
The butterfly that always abides.
The one who openly receives me with gladness.
Now, in my life I'm wondering,
I'm asking,
Ruth, will you be that one and only one?
Will you marry me?³

The sky is the limit when it comes to popping the question. In fact, if you'd like a few more ideas, you can go to our Web site at www.beforeyougetengaged.com and find a whole list of them there. If you're ready to get engaged, this is a very significant moment. However you do it, it's something you both will remember for the rest of your lives.

Whatever you do, I hope you won't find yourself someday saying what this guy said when he wrote, "I did very little to make it special or memorable. Oh, how I wish I could relive that one. My counsel to young men is invest the time and creativity to create a wonderful memory of the engagement."

I'd agree. After all you have been through to get to this moment, make it special. You have much to be thankful for.

Appendix A

● ADDITIONAL RESOURCES

Visit the Web site www.beforeyougetengaged.com to hear the rest of Brent and Danielle's story and to get additional help, including:

- Books
- Workbooks
- Video resources
- Teaching resources
- Ideas to help you pop the question

Appendix B
❯ SURVEY SAYS

In a recent survey conducted by Dave Gudgel, more than one hundred married couples were asked the following questions, with the following results:

1. What indicators did you use that convinced you it was time to get engaged? (114 responses)

   20%   I just knew it was the right person
   17%   The timing was right (financially and otherwise)
   13%   We believed it was God's will
   11%   Other's counsel and support
   6%   Shared values, interests, and goals

6%   We were in love

6%   We liked each other as friends

5%   We had spent plenty of time together

5%   We were ready to make an exclusive commit-
      ment to each other

4%   We felt peace in our hearts

4%   We were sexually struggling to remain pure

2%   We had strong communication and conflict res-
      olution

1%   Desire to escape loneliness

2. If someone asked you how to "know for sure" that they
   should ask someone to marry them, what suggestions
   would you give them? (109 responses)

20%   Look for shared values, goals, interests

15%   Pray

14%   Seek others' input (family, friends, counselor,
       pastor)

12%   Look for genuine love and unconditional com-
       mitment

9%   Make sure you are spiritually compatible

5%   Make sure you are close friends with a strong
       emotional connection

5%   You need transparent, honest communication

5%   You share mutual respect

4%   You have complete peace that this is the right
       one

4%   You can see mature character traits

4%   You've spent enough time getting to know each
       other (at least a year)

3%   Signs of unselfishness

3. What made how you got engaged special?
   (105 responses)

   42%   What he did to make it personal
   17%   It was at a special place
   10%   It took a lot of planning
   9%   It wasn't special
   8%   It happened on the spur-of-the-moment
   7%   It was a mutual decision
   7%   It was a special day (Valentine's Day, Easter, one-
         year dating anniversary, Groundhog Day)

4. How long did you and your spouse date each other
   before you got engaged? (123 responses)
   21 months average length

5. How long were you engaged before you got married?
   (119 responses)
   7 months average length

6. How long have you been married to this person?
   (116 responses)
   23 years average length

7. How old were you when you got married?
   (118 responses)
   26.5 years average age

About the Authors

DAVID GUDGEL

David Gudgel is the senior pastor at Bethany Bible Church and host of a thirty-minute weekday radio program in Phoenix, Arizona. A graduate of Westmont College, Talbot Theological Seminary, and Western Seminary, Dr. Gudgel is the author of *Before You Live Together.* He has been in vocational ministry for thirty-five years and, with his wife, Bernice, has three twenty-something children: one married, one not, and one (Brent) seriously thinking about it.

BRENT GUDGEL

Brent Gudgel is a filmmaker and photographer in Los Angeles. An owner of Chronicle Project, he directed the award-winning film *Dear Francis*, which aired on Showtime in 2007, and has worked on projects in more than twenty countries. When not on a set, Brent travels to conferences, colleges, camps, and churches across America to speak about social justice. He is currently considering popping the question.

DANIELLE FITCH

Danielle Fitch recently graduated from Azusa Pacific University. Her focus on English with a concentration in teaching allows her to continue in literary and educational endeavors, but her real love, besides Brent, is with international nonprofit organizations.

Notes

Introduction: Thinking about Engagement?

1. Dr. Bill Maier, *Focus on the Family* interview, "Why You Shouldn't Live Together," August 1, 2006.
2. Sylvia Weishaus and Dorothy Field, "A Half Century of Marriage: Continuity or Change?" *Journal of Marriage and the Family*, Vol. 50, No. 3 (August 1988): 763-74.
3. "Behind Closed Doors," A *Woman's Day* and AOL Survey (February 2007), http://www.womansday.com/home/11092/behind-closed-doors-a-womans-day-and-aol-survey.html.

Chapter 1: Would You Marry You?

1. Taken from *Relationships* by Dr. Les Parrott III, Leslie Parrott. Copyright © 1998 by Les and Leslie Parrott. Used by permission of Zondervan.
2. Ibid., 21.
3. 1 Samuel 25:3, 17.
4. 1 Samuel 25:3, 33.
5. 1 Samuel 25:32–35.
6. 1 Samuel 25:17, 25.
7. 1 Samuel 25:37–38.
8. Neil Clark Warren and Les Parrott, *Love the Life You Live* (Carol Stream: Tyndale House, 2003), 11.
9. Mark 12:30–31.
10. "Idiot Light," Wikipedia Encyclopedia, http://en.wikipedia.org/wiki/Idiotlight.
11. "Socrates," Wikipedia Encyclopedia, http://en.wikiquote.org/wiki/Socrates.
12. 1 Timothy 4:16 NASB.
13. "Augustine," Harvard Square Library, http://www.harvardsquarelibrary.org/Prayers/augustine.html (emphasis mine).
14. Ephesians 3:19 NASB.
15. John 10:10 (emphasis mine).
16. Galatians 5:22–23.
17. Galatians 5:14.
18. 1 Thessalonians 3:12 (emphasis mine).
19. 1 Corinthians 13:4–8.
20. Parrott, *Relationships*, 173.

21. "Compulsion for completion" is a term coined by Les and Leslie Parrott, who have helped my thinking on this subject.
22. Parrott, *Relationships*, 23.
23. Ibid., 128–29.
24. Romans 12:3.
25. Romans 15:13 (emphasis mine).

Chapter 2: Are You All Dated Out?

1. Genesis 29:1–20.
2. Genesis 29:17 NASB (emphasis mine).
3. Genesis 29:18.

Chapter 3: How Does "Till Death Do Us Part" Sound?

1. Matthew 19:3 MSG.
2. Matthew 19:6 NLT.
3. Matthew 19:10 NLT.
4. *The Antiquities of Josephus*, Volume 4, 253.
5. Cited in Dr. Abraham Cohen, *Everyman's Talmud* (London: J. M. Dent & Sons Ltd, 1932), 162.
6. Quoted in Ira Rifkin, "Love Makes Married Life Go 'Round—And Start All Over Again," *L.A. Life, Daily News*, Monday, November 26, 1984, 4.
7. Wedding vows exchange. http://www.beliefnet.com/uExp/ WeddingCeremonyDisplay.asp?PraiseId=45944&PraiseType=1&mode=dsp.
8. James W. Sweeney, "Prenuptial Papers Called Poor Sign," *Daily News* (June 25, 1985): 16.
9. Carlin Flora, "Let's Make a Deal: Does a Prenuptial Agreement Sow the Seeds of Divorce or Provide a Crash Course in Conflict Resolution?" *Psychology Today* (November–December 2004), http://www.findarticles.com/ p/articles/mim1175/is637/ain8585954.
10. Troy Thompson, "On Relationships: Finding Yourself, Finding a Place, Finding a Soul Mate," http://www.troyandjessica.com/article/33/romance/ finding-yourself-finding-your-soulmate.html.
11. Jon Meacham, "Pilgrim's Progress," *Newsweek*, August 14, 2000, 36.

Chapter 4: Is Now the Right Time or Not?

1. www.census.gov/population/socdemo/hh-fam/tabMS-2.pd.
2. Marcia and Tom Lasswell, *Marriage and the Family* (Belmont, CA: Waddsworth Publishing, 1987), 164.
3. Neil Clark Warren, *Finding the Love of Your Life* (Colorado Springs: Focus on the Family, 1998), 12.
4. Talmudists in the Jewish culture forbid marriage under the age of thirteen years and a day for men and twelve years and a day for women. Ezekiel 16:7–8 suggests that a marriageable age came somewhere after puberty. Metaphorically it says, "I made you grow like a plant of the field. You grew up and developed and became the most beautiful of jewels. Your breasts were formed and your hair grew, you who were naked and bare. Later I

passed by, and when I looked at you and saw that you were old enough for love, I spread the corner of my garment over you and covered your naked-ness. I gave you my solemn oath and entered into a covenant with you, declares the Sovereign LORD, and you became mine." The symbolic act of spreading the corner of the garment signified protection and betrothal. This happened sometime after puberty.

5.   Proverbs 5:18 (emphasis mine).
6.   1 Timothy 5:8.
7.   Deuteronomy 24:5 (MSG).
8.   http://www.marriagemissions.com/newlywed/men_first_year.php, http://www.marriagebuilders.com/graphic/mbi5038_qa.html.
9.   Matthew 19:11–12.
10.   1 Corinthians 7:9.

Chapter 5: Are You "In Love"?

1.   Steve Rogers, "Bachelor Couple Andrew Firestone and Jen Schefft Breakup," (December 9, 2003), http://www.realitytvworld.com/news/bachelor-couple-andrew-firestone-and-jen-schefft-breakup-2068.php.
2.   http://abclocal.go.com/wls/story?section=News&id=213392.
3.   From *The Truth About Love: The Highs, the Lows, and How You Can Make it Last Forever* by Pat Love, Ed.D. Copyright © 2001 by Patricia Love. Reprinted with the permission of Simon & Schuster Adlult Publishing Group.
4.   Ibid., 42–43.
5.   Aircraft Accident Report, Aloha Airlines, Flight 243, Boeing 737-200, N73711, near Maui, Hawaii, April 28, 1988, http://www.aloha.net/~icarus.
6.   Genesis 29:17–18.
7.   The Hebrew word used here is *ahab*, which is the love of sexual desire and emotional attachment. Merrill F. Unger, *Nelson's Expository Dictionary of the Old Testament* (Nashville: Thomas Nelson, 1980), 230–31.
8.   Song of Solomon 1:2.
9.   Song of Solomon 1:15–16.
10.   Sady Jo Smokey, "Leaky Shower Leads to Romance," *The Arizona Republic,* Arizona Living, Wednesday, January 3, 2007.
11.   Tommy Nelson, *The Book of Romance* (Nashville: Thomas Nelson, Inc., 1998), 2–3. Reprinted by permission. All rights reserved.
12.   Genesis 2:18.
13.   Ecclesiastes 4:9–10.
14.   1 Samuel 18:1 NASB.
15.   John 5:20.
16.   Interview conducted by Stan Guthrie, "What Married Women Want," *Christianity Today,* October 2006, 122.
17.   Ibid., 122.
18.   Ephesians 5:25.
19.   John 15:13.
20.   Ephesians 5:33.

Chapter 6: Do You Communicate Effectively?

1. James 1:19.
2. Ephesians 4:29.
3. James 4:1.
4. Proverbs 18:2.
5. Proverbs 12:15.
6. Proverbs 15:22.
7. Ecclesiastes 4:9.
8. Galatians 6:2.
9. Ephesians 4:15.
10. Ephesians 5:21.
11. Taken from *Why Am I Afraid to Tell You Who I Am?* by John Powell. Copyright © 1999. Used by permission of Zondervan.
12. Ibid., 13.

Chapter 7: Are You on the Same Page?

1. Reprinted with permission from iVillage.com.
2. Amos 3:3 NKJV.
3. http://docs.yahoo.com/info/values.
4. http://docs.yahoo.com/info/values/page2.html.
5. Genesis 2:24.

Chapter 8: Are You Spiritually Connected?

1. 1 Corinthians 7:39.
2. Deuteronomy 7:3–4.
3. Judges 3:6–7.
4. Psalm 127:1.
5. 2 Corinthians 6:14.
6. 2 Corinthians 6:14–16.

Chapter 9: Are You Better Together than Apart?

1. Genesis 2:18.
2. Genesis 2:18.
3. For a detailed description of these four personality types and a personal personality evaluation, go to www.leadingfromyourstrengths.com and click the Marriage tab and then the Marriage Insights button.

Chapter 10: What Does Your Heart Say?

1. Colossians 3:15.

Chapter 11: Consider What God Says

1. Kasamba, Expert Advice Live, http://www.kasamba.com.
2. Proverbs 2:6.
3. James 1:5.
4. 2 Peter 3:9 NKJV.
5. Ephesians 5:17–18.
6. 1 Thessalonians 4:3–4.